G000089545

WHAT EVERY GUN SHOULD KNOW

David & Charles' Fieldsports and Fishing Titles

THE ANGLING TIMES BOOK OF COARSE FISHING
  Allan Haines and Mac Campbell
ANIMAL TRAPS AND TRAPPING New Edition
  James A. Bateman
BEAGLING J. C. Jeremy Hobson
THE BEST OF DICK WALKER'S COARSE FISHING
  Edited by Peter Maskell
COARSE ANGLING WATERS David Tipping
FISHING FROM MY ANGLE Tales by Cyril Holbrook
FLY DRESSING I David J. Collyer
FLY DRESSING II David J. Collyer
FLY TYING METHODS Darrel Martin
FOWLER IN THE WILD Eric Begbie
FOX HUNTING The Duke of Beaufort
GAME COOKERY Angela Humphreys
GAMEKEEPER John Foyster and Keith Proud
GOOD SHOOTING J. E. M. Ruffer
THE GREAT SHOOTS Brian P. Martin
HUNTER'S FEN John Humphreys
HUNTING An Introductory Handbook R. W. F. Poole
JEMIMA PARRY-JONES' FALCONRY: Care, Captive
  Breeding and Conservation Jemima Parry-Jones
KEN WHITEHEAD'S PIKE FISHING Ken Whitehead
PURDEY'S; THE GUNS AND THE FAMILY
  Richard Beaumont
SHOOTING PIGEONS John Humphreys
THE SHOTGUN Macdonald Hastings
SPORTING BIRDS OF THE BRITISH ISLES
  Brian P. Martin
SPORTING GUN James Douglas
SUCCESS WITH SALMON Crawford Little
TRAINING SPANIELS Joe Irving
TROUT AND SALMON FISHING Edited by Roy Eaton
WOODLAND MANAGEMENT FOR PHEASANTS AND
  WILDLIFE Nigel Gray

WHAT EVERY GUN SHOULD KNOW

J. C. Jeremy Hobson

Line drawings by Clare Pavey

DAVID & CHARLES
Newton Abbot · London · North Pomfret (Vt)

To Peter and Nicholas Nutting,
who gave me my first single-handed keeper's job
and the opportunity to learn the finer points of keepering,
together with an understanding of nature
and how it works.

British Library Cataloguing in Publication Data
Hobson, J.C. Jeremy
What every gun should know.
1. Great Britain. Game birds. Shooting.
Amateur's manuals
I. Title
799.2'4'0941

ISBN 0-7153-9174-7

Typeset by Typesetters (Birmingham) Ltd,
Smethwick, West Midlands
and printed in Great Britain
by Billings & Sons Limited, Worcester
for David & Charles Publishers plc
Brunel House Newton Abbot Devon

Distributed in the United States by
David & Charles Inc
North Pomfret Vermont 05053 USA

Contents

1
The First Steps

If you wish to go trout fishing, it is necessary to have a thorough understanding of the water and the likely movements of the fish throughout the open season and to be reasonably proficient at casting a line. Without some knowledge, it is unlikely that the tyro will catch anything.

With the necessary financial wherewithal, an approach can be made to the local foxhound pack and a subscription paid for a season's hunting. First however, you must learn to ride and a horse capable of withstanding a day's hunting is, of necessity, a strong one. Without a thorough grounding in the basics of riding you will spend, at the very least, more time on the ground than jumping fences.

Anyone can pick up a gun and buy a day's shooting and it does not matter whether you make a kill or not throughout the day.

Unlike fishing, where the worst that can happen is that you lose your balance and fall in the water, or hunting where bad riding may result in the injury or death of the rider, the shooter with no knowledge or experience of a gun, the workings of a shoot, dangerous behaviour and its likely outcome, is a potentially fatal menace to himself, his fellow sportsmen, their dogs, beaters and anyone or anything connected with any aspect of a shooting day.

Shooting is a sport of infinite variety. With the exception of yachting and polo, it can also be the most expensive sport and, as such, is very prestigious. In the last decade, many businessmen have seen a tremendous rise in their salaries and consider that shooting is a hobby to be pursued. People in general are enjoying a higher standard of living and consequently have more surplus income which may tempt them to try anything from a day's pheasant shooting to renting ground from a farmer in order to deal with a few pigeons.

Traditionally, pheasant shooting was passed down in the family from father to son; the young men of the family would learn the rules from their father and would spend many hours gaining experience with the estate gamekeeper. If the young 'squire' was allowed to carry a gun while accompanying the keeper on his feeding and trapping rounds, under no circumstances would he have been allowed to put cartridges down the barrel until either the owner or the keeper was satisfied that the novice shooter was sufficiently competent to know exactly what was dangerous and what was not.

Shooting is now enjoying more popularity than ever before mainly because most landowners can no longer afford to keep their sport exclusively to themselves and need to offer their shooting facilities to the general public in order to raise some additional income. There is, therefore, adequate supply and demand but, as a general rule, the average age of newcomers to the sport is around thirty-five to forty. Picking up a gun for the first time at that age often means that much basic training has been missed and, without a full understanding of the sport, much enjoyment can also be missed.

Choosing a gun and some gun law

Surprisingly, there are very few laws concerning the sale and acquisition of a shotgun. In fact, according to the Firearms Act (1968), any person of seventeen years or over may purchase a shotgun provided that he also holds a valid shotgun certificate. Fifteen-year-olds may use shotguns without supervision provided that they, too, hold certificates, but it is against the law for fifteen-year-olds to attempt to buy either a gun or ammunition. Under the age of fifteen, it is an offence to have an assembled shotgun or for anyone to make a gift of a shotgun or ammunition to anyone under that age. There are, however, two exceptions: it is permissible for anyone under the age of fifteen to carry a shotgun in a cover provided that the gun cannot be fired, and for him to use and fire a gun if he is with someone over the age of twenty-one who possesses a valid shotgun certificate.

The words 'valid shotgun certificate' appear frequently in section 11 of the act. Without a valid shotgun certificate, a person is restricted to carrying a gun or ammunition provided that they do not fire the weapon, or they may '... borrow a shotgun from the occupier of private premises and use it on those premises in the occupier's presence'.

Subsection (6) permits a shotgun to be used '... at a time and place approved for shooting at artificial targets by the chief officer of police for the area in which that place is situated'.

Apart from age, there is no real reason why anyone should not have a shotgun certificate and there is no way that a chief officer of police can refuse to grant a certificate unless he has strong reason to believe that, for one reason or another, an applicant is prohibited under the act from possessing a shotgun, or cannot be permitted to possess a shotgun without causing danger to the general public safety or to the peace.

Having obtained the necessary shotgun certificate, choosing a suitable gun is the next step. Although selection is very much a matter of personal preference, the actual choice depends on three things: the money available, the type of shooting in which one expects to be involved and, to a lesser extent, the shooter's age, height and health.

Taking the latter subject first, an older person or a lady will shoot better with a lighter gun – say, a 20 or 16 bore – whereas the average shooter will prefer a 12 bore. Having said that, nowadays it is popular for even the strongest, healthiest person to use a 20 bore on the shooting field and, provided that the gun is correctly handled, there is no reason why it should not kill just as cleanly and efficiently as a 12 bore.

A word of warning

Never keep 20- and 12- bore cartridges together. A 20-bore cartridge will disappear into the breech of a 12 bore which will introduce an additional and potentially lethal danger, not only to fellow guns but most likely to yourself. The discharge of a 12-bore cartridge when a 20-bore is lodged further down the chamber has every chance of causing the barrel to blow out and taking away the side of your face.

Secondly, in general an ideal all-rounder's gun is one which is not so heavy that it causes your arms to tire by the end of the day nor yet so light that the recoil causes bruising to the shoulder. In the days when the landed gentry were the only people who had the time and money for shooting, they would have the shotgun for every occasion, ranging from a pair of specially built lightweight guns for shooting driven birds to wildfowling guns with a heavy shot load through 3in (76mm) chambers.

Today, there are also specialist clay-pigeon shooting guns with the barrels bored out for skeet and sporting layouts or more tightly choked for 'trap' and 'down the line'. These are unlikely to interest the purist game-shooter, who is also more likely to prefer a side-by-side gun rather than an over-and-under. It is not just the prestige attached to shooting with a side-by-side, for neither tradition nor appearances will make a person shoot well if the weapon is not suited to his physical attributes. The side-by-side is designed for game shooting and is therefore easier to swing on to high-flying pheasants, jinking grouse or hedge-hopping partridges.

Any gun must, of course, fit the shooter and so the distance from stock to trigger and how it compares with the buyer's arm length will have to be considered.

Although most people have a right 'master' eye, it is not uncommon for the left eye to take control when you bring the gun up to the target and if this is the case, it may be necessary to purchase a gun with a 'crossover' stock. Unless you are having a gun specially made, acquiring such a weapon could prove difficult, although you may be lucky enough to find a second-hand one. However, if the problem is not too severe, a good gunsmith may be able to alter the cast of a gun that he has already in stock.

I have deliberately left the question of gun prices until last because there is not much advice that can be given without knowing the individual's financial situation. Prices can vary from a few hundred pounds for a basic continental box-lock non-ejector to tens of thousands of pounds for a made-to-measure side-lock from one of the world's top gun manufacturers based in London or Birmingham. The shooter should spend as much as he can reasonably afford: apart from anything else, a well-constructed English gun will prove to be a sound investment and a valuable family heirloom. If a gun of this nature can be afforded, look out for one made between the two world wars, a time thought by many to have produced the best craftsmanship and quality.

Take good advice

No matter how much the gun costs, make absolutely certain that it has British proofmarks on the lumps and purchase it from a reliable and reputable company which is well known and used by other shooting enthusiasts. Better still, take someone with you who knows about shotguns and be guided by them, not by the fact that the gun has pretty engraving on the action.

The first steps

The successful businessman may be lucky enough to be invited to shoot on a top-class estate where a day or several days have been bought by a company in order to clinch certain deals, by way of a 'thank you' for a favour carried out in the office or to entertain clients from another firm who may eventually put business into the host's hands. It is unlikely that the person who can afford to pay for a 300–400 bird day will be interested in learning the basics of shooting, but if he has a genuine interest in all aspects of the sport, then perhaps he will.

A shooting school is the obvious answer to learning shooting skills. Many such schools exist, all with understanding and qualified instructors. Not only will the basic points of gun management and safety be explained, but there will be ample opportunity to test your skill at the varying types of sporting clay-pigeon targets. Although these targets supposedly simulate certain quarry species, they do not do so and, once thrown and past their zenith, they can only slow down, unlike a live bird or animal which goes faster and faster. Nevertheless, if you can begin to hit them in a consistent and methodical manner, the experience should stand you in good stead when it comes to shooting in the field.

Shooting schools are expensive and an hour's tuition will cost about £30, exclusive of the cost of clays and cartridges. Clay-pigeon shooting clubs are a cheaper alternative, but you must remember that there is no tuition.

Having spent several hours being coached, you may be lucky enough to get some rough shooting from a local farmer or landowner. Rough shooting on mixed terrain probably provides the greatest variety of sport, but that in itself is unlikely to satisfy the shooter for long. Soon, as your enthusiasm grows, nothing short of a day standing forward for driven pheasants will be good enough.

The Gun is now faced with several, expensive, alternatives: you can either buy or rent a sufficient number of acres to be able to stock the land with game and put a keeper in charge; you can rely on the occasional invitation from generous friends; or (probably the most likely choice) you can join a team of friends to set up a 'roving' syndicate.

A roving syndicate varies considerably. The more usual arrangement is for friends to share the cost of shooting on the same estate throughout the season. The syndicate merely finds a trustworthy letting agency and puts forward certain specifications. The system certainly leads to a greater variety of shooting: you have the advantage of picking and choosing what is on offer, shooting as few or as many birds as you like and selecting days that are convenient to you and not when the keeper or landowner determines; in addition, there is the opportunity to see different types of countryside without the risk of becoming bored at watching the same piece of woodland driven in the same way each week. There is also the choice of quarry species and a good agent should be able to find the syndicate some suitable grouse shooting in Scotland with as much ease as he can find prime pheasant shooting in Hampshire.

How sporting agencies work will be discussed in a later chapter but, basically, they make their money by taking a percentage from the shoot with days to let and from the potential shooter, and in return will guarantee to supply exactly what the guns require, from accommodation to advice as to how much to tip the keeper at the end of the day.

On being invited

You may be reading this book because you have expressed an interest in shooting to a friend who is in a position to offer you an invitation to shoot for a day. It used to be said that if you possessed a Land-Rover or a good working dog, there would be no shortage of invitations to shoot. Today, however, if you are fortunate enough to be a guest at a shoot, you must make sure that a second invitation follows as a result of your impeccable behaviour the first time round.

Traditionally, being a host means preparing a guest list as carefully as you would plan a successful dinner party. It is not merely a matter of shooting birds and inviting those people most likely to kill a good bag.

There are possibly one or two very rare occasions, however, when it might just be permissible to invite only those shooters who are likely to kill a good bag. For instance, if you own a grouse moor and intend to sell it in a year's time, then to be able to quote an excellent final season's bag will add a substantial sum to the asking price, but at any other time large bags should be a thing of the past and their revival will only damage the good reputation for which shooting has fought so long.

Hosting a shoot

You need not necessarily own a shoot in order to invite

your friends for a day's sport. A director whose company has bought a day via an agency may be responsible for inviting seven clients.

Among friends, a formal written invitation to a shoot is probably not necessary, but the good host will confirm a verbal invitation a few days before the occasion by means of a telephone call. During the course of the conversation, the host should give his guest as much information as possible: how many birds are likely to be shot (from which the guest can work out how many cartridges he will need), whether it will be pheasants only or, in the early part of the season, whether a few partridge or duck drives will be included. The host of a large shoot may expect his guests to bring a pair of guns; if they cannot find anyone willing to load the second gun, the host should enquire whether the guest will require a loader.

The host should also discuss eating arrangements because his guest might feel embarrassed if, at lunchtime, he returns to his car for his sandwiches only to be told by the butler that his presence is requested in the dining-room.

There are a few other points which the Gun should expect to be told if he is to avoid other embarrassments. Without knowing the form, turning up with five hundred cartridges and a new Savile Row suit on a day when the team is expected to walk all day rather than use a posse of beaters in order to drive birds forward to standing guns, can make the guest feel awkward and unable to enjoy his day. Conversely, taking an unruly gun-dog to a driven bird shoot will not endear its owner to either his host or the keeper, whereas on a rough shoot the animal could prove to be a useful asset. Clarify any doubtful points, no matter how simple they may seem.

Etiquette and gun safety

If you wish to be considered an old hand by more experienced members of the shooting party, it will be necessary to do more than drag your jacket through the mud and barbed-wire in an effort to age it. No matter how good a shot you may be, if you ignore the basic aspects of safety and etiquette on the shooting day, it is unlikely that you will receive many further invitations or that you will be considered a true member of the sporting fraternity.

There is a saying that the shooting world is a small one. The saying is used mainly in connection with keepers: if they are incompetent at their job or in any way dishonest, their reputation will reach a prospective employer before the keeper has even stuck a stamp on his letter of application. Nevertheless, the saying also applies to dangerous shooting and, if an experienced Gun sees someone guilty of irresponsible behaviour on an estate in Hampshire, that Gun might be shooting in Scotland the next week and be telling his host all about it. The crime is worsened each time the story is told until, by the time the tale reaches a shoot in Shropshire where the guilty party may be a guest, his host may find himself having to make excuses in order to turn the dangerous shot away and fill his place with someone of a more trustworthy nature. This is an extreme example, perhaps, but it illustrates the potential damage to a person's reputation.

In an effort to avoid being branded a dangerous shot, the new Gun should consider several points before venturing out onto the shooting field. Never forget that shooting is meant to be a sport and that it is not the intention to kill every bird. If this were the case, the keeper could do the job far more simply and inexpensively when the poults are on the rearing field rather than put in a great deal of time and effort in producing strong, high-flying pheasants.

The desire to get your money's worth may be strong if you are paying for your day's shoot, but if a return for the money is all that is required, you could fill several freezers by handing over the cost of the day to a game-dealer and asking him to supply a quantity of oven-ready pheasants.

You must respect the quarry, therefore. One of the reasons for writing this book is to prevent the shooter from viewing the bird or mammal as a mere target – it is a living creature and as such deserves as much respect as you would give a human being.

It is, or should be, the ambition of every shooting man and woman to kill the quarry as quickly and as cleanly as possible. Unfortunately (and this may be the result of an inexperienced

Gun shooting at a bird too far away), on every shooting day a proportion of gamebirds will be pricked and need to be dispatched as humanely as possible on being collected. The quickest method is to break the bird's neck by holding the body in one hand and pulling the head downwards at right angles with the other hand – the vertebrae will be dislocated, causing instant death. Although this method is humane and is thus used without exception by chicken breeders, it does, however, cause problems when the bird is hung on the game cart or in the game larder. A combination of body weight and, in the case of the game cart, a bumpy homeward ride, is likely to cause the head and body to part company.

An alternative method would be to purchase (and carry with you at all times) a small 'priest' as used by game

Although probably the most effective and humane way of dispatching a wounded bird, breaking the neck can cause unnecessary damage to the carcase and even result in the head separating from the body. Cosmetic and financial aspects should, however, take second place to a quick kill

fishermen to kill their catch. This is so much easier than pulling the gun-peg number out of the ground and hitting the bird to death with it or locating a tree or fence stake and repeatedly battering the pheasant's head against it. Old-time keepers had other methods of dispatching game: I have seen one keeper bite the bird's skull and another, on the grouse moor, take a primary feather from the wing and pierce it through the bird's ear orifice, presumably causing death by brain damage.

Before moving off at the start of the day, the host may like to give a pre-shoot briefing on the subject of safety. This talk should not be necessary, but it gives an opportunity to explain that there should be no shooting at ground game and to give the local opinion regarding foxes. Some hosts are also members of the hunt and like to leave the foxes to provide sport for others.

The pre-shoot briefing would also be a good time to explain the positioning of stops and flankers or where the neighbouring Guns will be if there is anything at all unexpected about a

Grouse shooting is possibly the most potentially dangerous form of sport available. In an effort to prevent the occupant swinging through the line, it is a good idea to insert two pegs, one on either side of the butt

particular drive. When grouse shooting, this information can, on occasions, be absolutely vital as grouse driving is probably the most dangerous of any of the types of shooting available. It is far too easy for even the experienced shot to become disorientated and shoot down the line when he cannot see his next man in a dip or over the brow of a hill. For this reason, the Gannocky safety-pin is a good idea: when a pair is correctly inserted in the butt at points to the right and left of the Gun, he will be prevented from swinging through the line.

Before leaving the meeting point, peg numbers will be given out. After selecting one, you should remember it and change accordingly after each drive. Most estates move up two after every stand which, in theory, gives everyone the opportunity of at least one good peg on the day. I make a point of asking each Gun to remember his number as it frequently happens that even the most adept businessman fails to find his correct peg after the second or third drive of the day and so wastes time which could be used for sport.

Once at the peg, you should carefully gauge the safety zones and the likely direction from which the birds will fly. When they do come, shoot only those which are definitely yours. Taking a pheasant from another Gun is a heinous crime and nothing is more aggravating to the neighbouring Gun who sees a bird, sets himself up and is ready to pull the trigger, and then finds the bird already tumbling towards him. Shooting matters are not always clear-cut and, in some drives, birds crossing over a right-hand Gun are his momentarily. If this is the case, shoot a few and let a few through, especially those that look like offering a better shot a few seconds later. When a bird has been missed, then obviously fellow Guns are entitled to shoot at it.

Similar action needs to be taken when, either because a drive has a small heading or because the main bulk of the birds fly over only one or two Guns, it is necessary to double-bank your Guns. If you are fortunate enough to have drawn a peg in the front row, remember to let a few birds through to those waiting patiently behind.

There is no excuse for dangerous shooting when pheasants are the quarry. If they are flying low, do not shoot them, thus avoiding any near-misses. Beaters no longer accept being shot at as an excellent joke and personal compliment combined, as seems to have been the case in 1911 when an old family retainer remarked, 'Oh lor, the master's got me again.'

Swinging through the line to attempt to shoot a bird which was too low as it emerged from the cover has three potential danger points: at the time it leaves the woods at beaters' head level; as it skims across a neighbouring Gun's head, and as it tries to land in the cover immediately behind the line where pickers-up are probably placed. No one, you might think, would shoot at such a non-sporting bird, but I can assure you that they do. I well remember picking up on a local shoot and at the end of the drive being asked by one of the Guns whether I had managed to pick up a particular bird. Upon telling him that I had, he replied, 'Oh well done, I wasn't sure whether I'd hit it or it had knocked itself out on the barbed-wire fence!'

Today, there are possibly as many as ten times more people shooting as there were before the last war and, with incidents such as the above, it is perhaps surprising that not more injuries occur on the shooting field.

Safety

If someone notices that a fellow Gun has been handling his weapon dangerously, he should raise the matter with him as soon as possible and also have a word with the host or shoot manager. Any embarrassment which this may cause will be far outweighed by the knowledge that it may have prevented an accident.

On an organised day, you should never shoot between drives and you should carry your gun empty, preferably in a canvas sleeve. The canvas sleeve protects the weapon when you are climbing through a fence or scrambling into the back of a Land-Rover or up onto a tractor and trailer, and it is also reassuring for fellow Guns that, in the sling, the gun is almost sure to be empty. Basically, then, the gun should remain unloaded at all times, except when you are anticipating the imminent appearance of your quarry. This is easy to judge when you are standing at a peg listening to the tapping of the beaters, but not so easy when you are lying on the foreshore waiting for duck. In the latter case, discipline must be imposed in accordance with your own judgement.

There are some experienced Guns who feel that it is unnecessary to break their gun between drives. They will obviously have removed the cartridges from the chambers as soon as the keeper has blown his whistle to signal the end of the drive and believe that, by leaving the gun broken, it may get damaged or, on a wet or snowy day, go rusty internally as a result. Having the gun open means that fellow guests can see that there are no cartridges left inside and they do not need to worry about being shot in the feet.

A word of warning!
A gun should *never*, at any time, point at anyone.

What happens if an accident occurs depends on several things. A person who sells a day's shooting will adopt a different, more lenient attitude than the host on a private shoot when it is possible for anyone to transgress. The lenient attitude of the businessman is to encourage his clients to return to another shoot – preferably with their friends. Some people believe that a dangerous shot on whatever kind of day should be sent home immediately and if he has paid for the day, then his money should be forfeited. One thing is certain: he will not have the sympathy of his fellow Guns.

It is permissible to shoot low birds when a bird is obviously pricked or otherwise wounded from another day. Even so, great care must be taken not to create a danger to other Guns and the various shoot attendants. A slow, wounded bird is not the easiest thing to hit and I have, on many occasions, called out from the beating line, 'Shoot that bird – it's pricked' only to hear a shot ring out and see the target continue unscathed. All may not necessarily be lost, however, and I have taken the dogs out the following day and picked up the bird where it landed or have been able to capture it a few days later as it hobbled back to the feed ride.

Tipping the keeper

Unlike most workers on the land, the keeper cannot expect to be paid overtime even though he may be working a fourteen-hour day during the busy season of rearing and releasing. It can be argued that the situation will balance out and that, even though he may be fully employed for two or three months, there will be another two or three months at the end of the season when he will be quite slack. Although this is true, the fact remains that the keeper's salary is unlikely to do more than pay for his weekly grocery bill and a few extras for the house. It is not possible for a keeper to save money or to pay a mortgage for a house which he may need upon retirement when he no longer has the security of a tied cottage. The keeper's tips form a vital part of his income and HM Inspector of Taxes knows this and expects the keeper to add them to his total income. In my opinion, it is wrong to have to rely on such gratuities paid by guests of the shoot, especially when, perhaps through no fault of his own, the day's events do not go well and the keeper's tips reflect this.

The Gun should know that it is not absolutely necessary to tip the keeper if it is felt that he has produced a mediocre day when, with a little more effort, results could have been much better. Indeed, it would be hypocritical to tip. When you have had a good day (and not merely due to the size of the bag), a tip will show your appreciation and offering it will give the Gun an opportunity to thank the keeper and to discuss the day's events. Again, it is all a question of good manners and etiquette.

The Gun should arrive in the morning with his tip ready prepared. It is embarrassing to the keeper to be asked to change a note or to see the Guns in a huddle deciding how much to tip and swopping notes between themselves. Apparent spontaneity is preferable to carrying out the procedure with bad grace.

Keepers who work for syndicates have told me of a tendency for its members to pool the season's tips at Christmas or at the end of the season rather than give them to the individual keeper, thereby missing the opportunity to thank the keeper on a personal basis which, after all, is the whole point of tipping.

Insurance

Every shoot will, or certainly should, be insured for any accident or eventuality which may occur on the shooting day and the types of insurances available will be discussed in greater detail in the following chapter. Even so, it will be an irresponsible person who neglects to cover himself for third-party liability. To help with this, membership of the British Association for Shooting and Conservation (BASC) automatically includes third-party liability cover of up to £1 million. Among its many benefits, the association also offers a legal service and advice shop.

Private insurance companies also offer such facilities but probably not at the same favourable rates as the BASC. It matters not with whom you insure but it is important that you are insured. No Gun should go onto the shooting field, be it for game or clay 'busting', without insuring himself. A weapon may be insured against damage or theft, but not even a top-class London-made gun is worth the life of a fellow sportsman.

2

The Gun Without A Shoot

Today, the Gun has more options available to him than ever before. You do not even need to possess a regular shooting venue to enjoy the best of what this country has to offer. Fortunately, there are many estate owners who wish to continue the lifestyle of their predecessors, but who cannot comfortably afford to do so without making some aspects of their good fortune available to the general public.

Owners of stately homes may open their houses to the general public, but it is more likely that the majority of landowners will merely attempt to offset some of their day-to-day running costs by selling a few sporting opportunities. By doing so, they can have a few 'private' days at cost rather than struggling to pay for their enjoyment. Because of present farming trends and restrictions, shooting is likely to become more available as a means of creating additional income for estate owners. Consequently, the shooter becomes the lucky recipient of several alternatives.

Hotels in prime sporting locations have seen the value of

buying or renting shooting rights from neighbouring landowners and can now offer almost any type of shooting to their residents.

A telephone call to any agency which advertises in the sporting press will probably result in the caller being offered a day or a week shooting his chosen quarry species on the dates he requires, either as an individual paying an eighth of the day's total costs or by paying for the whole day and inviting seven friends along.

You could rent part of a large estate, form a syndicate, employ a keeper and put down birds, but as the cost of renting a decent shoot with the facilities for housing a keeper and with the potential for providing both quality and quantity could be as much as £20 per acre in the South-east, you would need to have ample cash available. At the other end of the scale, the Forestry Commission offers sporting rights for as little as £2–3 per acre but, because of its planting policies, the ground is unlikely to offer more than a few days' enjoyable rough shooting and it is very doubtful whether it would be worth the shoot to employ a keeper and to release birds onto ground which is, as a general rule, unsuitable for game.

A fourth, very new, alternative is time-share shooting whereby estate agents can offer, on the instructions of the landlord, a 'syndication of pheasant shooting for up to eight Guns'. How the system works will vary from agent to agent and from estate to estate, but a few general points likely to prove common factors may be helpful to the shooter bereft of any shooting.

Time-share shooting

Under a time-share arrangement, the seller would probably be totally responsible for the full management of the shoot, employing and housing the keeper(s), providing him with transport, paying the beaters and providing accommodation for the night prior to and during the shoot. Costs would probably not include cartridges, tips and personal insurance including shoot cancellation because of bad weather. Additional accommodation for extra guests would probably be charged initially as an extra, but it could be charged annually at a fixed rate after agreements have been drawn up.

It is unlikely that time-share shooting would be offered in perpetuity but would occur perhaps for a term of, say, five or ten years. The number of days' shooting available would depend on the size of the estate which is offering the deal and the numbers of birds that are released.

Time-share example

One particular estate in Scotland offers time-shares 'For sale as a whole or by Gun for two consecutive days' shooting for nine years, including accommodation. Offers from £8,606 per Gun.' The buyer can take his two days in November, December or January and the estate adjusts its prices to take into account the expected higher bags in November and lesser ones in January. Obviously, VAT is added to the total price.

It must be difficult to forecast sport in future years and the person interested in time-share shooting must read all the small print and ask some searching questions. There must, for instance, be a guarantee from the estate that it will continue to release approximately the same numbers of birds in future years, and that it has made provision for the collapse and possible sale of whole or part of the estate which might be due either to financial problems or the death of the owner.

If bags decline and a particular season produces less birds than anticipated, the buyer could end up with a very poor deal unless this possibility has been written into the contract. To avoid the possibility of disappointment, it must be stated by the vendor that the difference between the bag that is actually attained and that which was promised should be refunded. An exceptionally good season could, however, mean that the owner is at a disadvantage, so the contract should also state that, if the actual totals are greater than those anticipated, the difference will be charged to the shooter at the current season's rates.

Because time-share shooting involves a considerable investment of money, it would be very foolish to take up a time-share offer without viewing the estate and the hosts should offer the opportunity to watch at least a day's shooting before any deal is signed. Talk to the keeper as well as to the owner and satisfy yourself that he appears to be competent and enthusiastic. If you get the opportunity to visit on a shooting day, notice how the keeper speaks to the Guns and handles his beating line.

The ground itself is obviously important and you can look forward to some interesting and enjoyable days if the land is undulating and contains small, manageable woodlands and plenty of game-cover crops. An ideal ground would be 80 per cent arable and 20 per cent woodland, the latter being split rather than being in one large wood. However, even flat and apparently uninteresting ground can produce surprisingly good sport if it is handled by a knowledgeable keeper.

Agencies and how they work

The development of both hotel-based shooting holidays and commercial sporting agencies suggests an increase in the marketing of sporting shooting and, for the Gun who does not wish to burden himself with the day-to-day running of a shoot, an agency is definitely a good idea. The benefits and excitement of forming a roving syndicate have already been explained in Chapter 1, but the sportsman who has enough organising in his business life, and wishes to take himself and his wife away for the weekend and escape the pressures of modern life, need only telephone the agency representative and give the minimum of facts as to time, date, type of shooting and accommodation requirements and leave the rest to him.

There is, however, a worrying tendency for commercial shooting days to be sold by the bird or, worse still, by the cartridge. The latter phenomenon is utter commercialism, which has no regard for the environment or the keeper's hard work. It conjures up a picture of the Gun standing by his peg, seeing a bird and hurriedly checking the depth of his pocket before pulling the trigger. At least one estate where this form of shooting (it cannot be called sport) is carried out charges £3 (1987/88 season) per cartridge, irrespective of the number of birds shot.

Briefly, the way this type of commercial shooting works is this: the Gun turns up with all the paraphernalia of the shooting day but minus cartridges. These he buys from the estate and he can decide how many to purchase by assessing his financial position. If he finds himself out of cartridges by lunchtime, then he can see the keeper and buy some more. The cartridges are labelled with the name of the shoot to eliminate the risk of individuals smuggling in their own. At the end of the day, the Gun has two choices: he can return unspent cartridges and expect a refund, or take any remainders home.

Beware

Taken too far, commercial shooting can have a serious effect on the moral basis of the sport. As this kind of shooting is becoming more common, it is up to agency owners to ensure that the integrity of shooting is maintained.

Although not necessarily a good thing, the size of bag generally indicates the amount of money which the Gun is expected to pay but, conversely, the agency can offer no guarantee as to the number of birds shot as the total bag will depend on the skill of the Gun. If the birds are presented but the participants fail to shoot them, the daily charge must apply without refund. If, on the other hand, the shoot fails to present enough birds for the expected bag to be achieved, pro rata charges will apply.

The aim of any agency should be to arrange shoots and shooting holidays specifically designed to suit the clients. Individuals should receive the same attention as a full team and anyone who wishes to arrange something special, such as a very big day or a double-gun day for their friends, must not be treated any differently. Such individuals will, however, need to complete their reservation as early as possible to allow for forward planning.

A 50 per cent deposit normally confirms any telephone or written arrangements, but all account balances should be cleared well before the date of the shoot.

The going rate for commercial shooting at 1987–8 prices

is £15 a bird. Agency prices will vary according to the locality and reputation of the shoot but, whatever the price, it should include at least a simple lunch and, apart from the keeper's tip, no other supplementary costs should apply. Check these details before signing anything, otherwise you could find yourself paying £15 per individual quarry species and still have to pay for beaters and lunchtime drinks, arrangements for which appear in the small print so that no redress is allowed.

It is possible to arrange a long weekend shoot or, indeed, a holiday package. The latter offers four or five nights' accommodation, inclusive of bed and breakfast. The choice of hotel will influence the cost of the shoot and obviously you can expect to pay more if minor diversions such as swimming-pools, jacuzzis or a gymnasium are on offer. Again, take care when reading through the agent's literature as the prices quoted may only be for the shooting fees. If this is the case, the cost of a hotel for five nights' bed and breakfast could vary from £100 to £300 depending on its standards.

It is sometimes possible to take advantage of winter breaks offered by many hotels throughout the shooting months. The price usually includes two days' driven shooting and three nights' accommodation, with non- shooting companions charged for accommodation only.

Most agencies prefer to offer a basic programme which is designed to present different types of shoot days, planned for individual Guns to make up a team for the day. Anyone wishing to take along a full team and wanting either a smaller or larger day than is the norm can usually be accommodated, provided that sufficient notice is given to avoid interfering with existing reservations. A discount may then be given for a group booking.

Although charges vary from agency to agency, and the cost of rearing birds and putting on a shoot increases annually, it may be of some use to include one particular agency's prices in order to give the reader some indication of what a day is likely to cost. The agency in this example is Cowley Shooting Associates Ltd, the offices of which are in Crediton, Devon. For the 1987–8 shooting season the price guide for an eight-Gun team was as follows:

100-bird day = £1,650 – £206 per Gun
150-bird day = £2,475 – £310 per Gun
200-bird day = £3,300 – £410 per Gun

Agencies exist not simply to supply the requirements of wealthy shooters but also to offer 'walked-up' shooting. By doing so, the newcomer can even find himself on the grouse moors and, if the Gun is content to enjoy a simple and informal day's sport, with a fair chance of firing a few shots and coming home with a brace or two in the bag, it can be done – and without distressing the bank manager! Despite habitat losses in Scotland and poor breeding seasons in Yorkshire, there are still huge areas of the country which maintain reasonable grouse stocks and can afford some good sport for those who are prepared to do some walking. Agencies and sporting hotels have been quick to realise this and can provide the newcomer with some exciting, informal shooting without the cost being too high.

Walked-up days may vary in price if the Gun can bring his own dog. If not, the cost of supplying a working animal (plus, of course, its handler) would have to be met by the Guns.

Again, purely as an example, Cowley Shooting Associates Ltd require a team of at least four Guns who should bring with them at least two working dogs. The cost, provided that they shot at least twenty head of game, would have been £82 each during the 1987-8 season. The bag in this example includes all game shot but, for whatever reason, not picked up on the day.

Of necessity, the agencies' literature cannot cover every eventuality and may seem formal and unforgiving. The shooter has certain rights and expectations, however, and, as he is paying for a service, the agency needs to uphold certain standards.

Arrangements must be made between an agency representative and the owner of the shoot to ensure that potential Guns will not feel used and merely a means of earning easy money. It can, for instance, be aggravating to have shot nearly the expected total bag by lunchtime and then to be asked to stand around in the afternooon for three drives where only a dozen birds may be shot. The team should be given the alternative of finishing at lunchtime when the day's bag has been achieved or of shooting some better drives and paying for the extra birds shot. Above all, the agency should ensure a good deal: if 200 head has been bought, then 225 should be realised.

It matters little whether the shoot is providing a day for paying sportsmen or the keeper is supplying his employer's guests with an ordinary day; the format for the day should include at least three good drives – preferably the first one of the day (although this is not essential), secondly the one before lunch because this is the one which is talked about over pre-prandial drinks, and thirdly the last drive of the day, on which the shoot's reputation is set and the keeper's tip determined!

The sad fact is that many commercial shoots find themselves trapped by ever-increasing costs and offer their services to agencies who must determine certain rules and regulations to ensure that their reputation and that of shooting as a whole does not suffer. The most likely bone of contention between the public and those who shoot is probably the bag size. An example is the hue and cry in the press when members of the Royal Family meet annually at Christmas and are photographed out on the shooting field. The caption usually makes some mention of the bag at the end of the day and the paper's letters' page carries correspondence condemning the 'slaughter' for several editions.

Bag sizes

Although bag size is generally a taboo subject, the belief that it is the quality of the birds and not the quantity that matters is quite wrong and the same person who prides himself on shooting only high-flying, testing birds would soon become disgruntled if he had only a dozen screamers to fire at and the adrenalin was never allowed to flow because he was never present when a flush of perhaps a hundred birds flew over his head. In such a situation, it matters not to the average shooter whether a pheasant is high; instinct takes over and the trigger finger itches to pull and make contact.

When I have been unable to attend a friend's shooting day to give him a hand beating, I know that when I ring him up in the evening to see how he fared and ask 'if he has had a good day', the answer is likely to be, 'Oh, not bad – the Guns shot well and we ended up with 350.'

I have also heard Guns who shoot at least four times a week during the season compare notes:

'How did you get on at Fred Bloggs' on Monday?'

'Smashing day, we killed a record bag you know – that keeper of his certainly knows how to rear birds.'

'Oh good, I've got an invite there next month. Hope you left a few birds.'

Very rarely does one hear the comment, 'Oh we didn't see that many but what came over were absolute corkers.'

Employers are often guilty of double standards. During their pre-shoot walkabout, they insist that their keeper includes a certain drive because 'it's worthwhile even if only half a dozen birds come over' but, on the Sunday morning following a shoot when the keeper and the owner are discussing the good and bad points of the previous day, the employer will often comment, 'Oh, West Wood was all right – I shot a good bird – but it's a pity that you didn't show more pheasants. The Prince of Timbuctoo never got a shot, you know.' The keeper, if he is of normal keepering material, is immediately thrown into the depths of despondency and begins to worry as to the security of his job once the season draws to a close.

Attitudes to sport have changed, but it is not the fault of agencies or hotels. They are only reacting to a market demand brought about by a new breed of shooting person.

Sadly, not all game-shooters are interested in the countryside and, as they are paying for the day, they understandably want good value for money. I know that this is true from personal experience: although I have never paid for a day's game shooting, I have on many occasions paid £15.20 for a day's trout fishing and I have felt very frustrated when I have not caught the amount of fish that my money allowed me to take, whether it was due to the summer 'dog days' or merely to my own ineptitude. Fortunately, the estate on which I now work has a series of ponds suitable for stocking with game fish and my son and I have our own private fishing which we can attend whenever the mood takes us. The whole situation has now changed and if we spend an unproductive evening there is no pressure or incentive to catch our money's worth.

Unfortunately, many shooters who expect good value for money cannot tell the difference between a sparrow-hawk and a pigeon or a nut-hatch and a sparrow. I hope that, after reading the chapter on bird identification and game law (see Chapter 7), this criticism will not apply to the readers of this book but, nevertheless, there are many shooters who wish to do nothing more than pay their money and expect a good day's sport in return.

This attitude does not always work. The responsibility of having too many birds in order to ensure an adequate supply and demand can leave both keeper and owner dissatisfied. Both the keeper and owner have different ideals but, whatever their intentions, there is a capacity limit to the number of birds an area can hold. It is a simple matter of attitudes and education and, unless shooters are prepared to be less greedy regarding bag sizes, the well-being of game shooting is in danger.

On the other hand, the fact that so many people who want to achieve a large bag can afford to indulge their interest only ensures the further welfare of shooting activities and leaves the situation open for those who wish to take advantage of what a sporting hotel has to offer.

Sporting hotels

Contacting a sporting hotel with a view to organising (or, rather, getting the proprietors to organise) a day's shooting is an even better proposition than taking advantage of what an agency has to offer. Someone else is doing all the hard work and, having made your choice, it is not even necessary to worry about accommodation as it is part of the deal.

Another advantage (with the possible exception of grouse shooting) is the fact that the shooting can only be obtained outside the main tourist season, when hotels are offering special breaks and discounts.

Finding a reputable hotel which will cater for your individual requirements is another matter. Obviously, the best course is to rely on recommendations from fellow shooters who have enjoyed what a particular establishment has to offer but, apart from advertisements in the sporting press or the annual list of hotels published in the *Shooting Times and Country* magazine, a number of other sources of information are available from which you can acquire some addresses and telephone numbers.

Possibly because of the increasing financial problems of farmers who need to consider alternative uses for their land, many tourist boards are showing a keen interest in attracting the visiting sportsman. Some tourist boards, however, do show a certain reluctance to promote shooting facilities because of public opinion towards the killing of animals and birds purely for sport.

Many hotels offer vast acres over which to shoot. Indeed, the Lake Vyrnwy Hotel in Wales boasts shooting over some 18,000 acres, some of which is formal and some only rough.

There should be more scope for the marketing of walked-up or rough shooting to which many sportsmen are turning as a cheap alternative. Although the direct income is not likely to be as high as that which can be expected from an established game shoot, the less intensive management required can be beneficial only from the point of view of initial outlay. Therefore, a hedge which is likely to produce only two or three pheasants can be driven on a rough day and the Guns will be more than happy, whereas the same hedge and the same results would create much dissatisfaction among shooters standing forward on a formal day.

Catering for the sportsman involves a great deal of work for the hotel owner. As well as the normal day-to-day running of the establishment, there are also shooting leases to be kept up to date, rearing programmes to consider (where birds are released) and, perhaps most important, an environment suitable for the welfare of future game stocks to be maintained. Any commercial shooting venture needs to give plenty of thought to the future: it is all too easy to milk an estate dry by making money for a few years. The time may come, however, when there is no sport to enjoy, especially when no keeper is employed and no rearing programme is carried out.

Fortunately, at least one such establishment, the Lake Vyrnwy, shows fore-thought and details of the 1986–7 season are as follows:

> In the past we have been able to offer one or two walking-up and driven days of grouse. Over the last few years, along with most other places, the grouse have been declining alarmingly. Having taken advice from the Game Conservancy Council and the RSPB, we have decided to not shoot the moors for two seasons. We hope that this will allow the grouse time to recover to a sufficient level in three years' time.

Where it is impossible to stock artificially (as is the case of grouse), great care must be taken, especially when the hotel offers such diversities as driven snipe and woodcock shooting. Conducted responsibly, however, there is no reason why a hotel should not put such attractions forward to potential guests as well as the more usual days of driven pheasant or rough shooting when a mixture of pheasant, duck, pigeon, woodcock, snipe and rabbits can be expected.

The Arundell Arms (Lifton, Devon), one of England's leading sporting hotels, is a case in point and it offers a wide range of shooting and stalking holidays. There can be few establishments that are able to offer four days of driven snipe, possibly the most challenging of all forms of shooting. The bags obviously depend upon the accuracy of the Guns but, as an average, you can expect to have to shoot seven cartridges for each bird that is brought down. Being migrating birds, nothing is certain and individual drives can vary from a handful to several hundred birds that are put over the guns.

Five nights' accommodation (with private bath and all meals) in the 1987–8 season would have cost you £438 per Gun inclusive of VAT. For this you could have expected four days' actual shooting, plus any transport necessary to the relevant drives. A non-shooting partner would have been charged £215.

Many hotels also cater for the complete tyro, no matter

what his chosen field of sport. There are, for example, those who can organise a day with the local hound packs, fishing tuition on a trout river or perhaps some clay-shooting practice prior to a day at game.

It is also possible to acquire some knowledge in preparation for the forthcoming season and, if gun-dogs are your particular interest, the Salston Hotel (Exeter, Devon) has, for several years, been offering a gun-dog training weekend where practical water-work on the river and dummy retrieves, jumping practice and 'running rabbits' will show up the faults of both handlers and their dogs which will then, it is hoped, be rectified with the help of two experienced gun-dog trainers. The weekend consists of lectures, practical demonstrations, social get-togethers and discussions. The cost per person (plus dog) is currently around £150 and includes private bathroom, all meals and tuition.

Several excellent sporting establishments exist, notably in Scotland and the West Country where all types of formal and informal sport are on offer.

With sufficient funds, you would never need to leave a place like the Lake Vyrnwy Hotel where good fishing can be had throughout the summer months and a great variety of shooting during the winter. The Arundell Arms is perhaps a little unusual in being able to offer deer stalking in addition to some excellent shooting and fishing. The shooting of either red or roe deer is normally carried out from high seats, but individuals can, if they wish, stalk on foot. (A rifle of a calibre to fire a bullet of 150 grains is required for red deer stalking.)

Prices and insurance

Normally, most establishments request a non-returnable deposit per Gun on confirmation of a booking. In certain circumstances, however – for instance, if more than eight weeks' notice is given – it may be possible to have your deposit returned if it is necessary to cancel your previous booking. The amount required for a deposit may vary from £50 to 50 per cent of the total cost, so it is as well to be absolutely sure that you wish to make a firm booking before risking the loss of hard-earned cash.

It is possible to take out insurance against the possibility of having to cancel a booking and it is also as well to check whether the hotel has its own insurance against cancellation due to weather conditions. If not, you are strongly advised to see that this is included in your own cancellation policy.

All Guns, whether they are applying to an agency or to a hotel, must normally confirm that they have a valid shotgun licence, game licence and third-party indemnity (usually somewhere between £500,000 and £1 million).

Anyone resident in the United Kingdom must have a valid shotgun certificate, but overseas visitors do not require an English shotgun licence if they are in the country for thirty days or less during the preceding twelve months. Overseas visitors do, however, require a firearms certificate when stalking and this can normally be obtained for them by the agency or hotel provided that they give at least two months' notice. Confirmation that a Gun has all the required documents will normally be asked for in writing well before the date of the holiday.

During the inevitable correspondence, you should check the hotel's ability to keep your guns in a safe place – under the bed will not do. If the proprietors do not have a strongroom and therefore cannot hold themselves liable in the event of loss or damage, you should ensure that your personal insurance covers your gun while you are away from home.

3
What To Wear

What the Gun wears for his shooting excursions will depend greatly on which aspect of the sport he has chosen to pursue.

The grouse shooter in August is often able to shoot quite comfortably in shirt sleeves, 'plus-twos' and a pair of leather shoes, whereas the duck shooter on the marshes in late January requires all the warmth and weatherproofing he can get from his clothing. Before discussing the most suitable clothing for each aspect of the sport, there are certain requirements which should be common to the garments of all would-be shooters, the most important of which must be freedom of movement.

Plus-fours were probably the first item of clothing designed specifically with the shooting person in mind and they were made to correct several points which ordinary trousers failed to fulfil. Because of the vast amount of material contained in a pair of plus-fours, they gave the wearer a tremendous amount of freedom of movement which meant that striding over the heather or clambering through a cleft-and-rail fence on the partridge manor became much easier. Long trousers inevitably became dirty around the bottoms and any fashion accessories such as turn-ups were filled with grass-seed. Because wellingtons or other footwear which would prevent this problem did not exist, it was easier to wash a pair of woollen stockings than it was to clean a pair of trousers after each outing.

Apparently (and the only pair of true plus-fours that I have ever seen were worn by the head-keeper with whom I started my career) at least $1^1/_2$ft (45cm) of material was gathered around each knee. When the game shooter could no longer be carried by pony and trap to his peg and instead had to walk the remaining distance, his voluminous trousers inevitably became caught up in the ground cover. Developments were made in the design of trousers for game shooters and the improved product became known as 'plus-twos' because they contained half the original amount of cloth. They are still available today but are usually called shooting breeches when they are bought off the peg. Modern plus-twos are still designed with a generous cut and, if made of pure cotton cloth plus-twos are suitable for any kind of shooting.

Jackets and coats need the same criteria: thick clothing will increase the length of gun stock needed, less clothing will decrease it. A wildfowler in heavy winter clothes has less freedom of movement with his gun than has a midsummer pigeon shooter who is lightly clad. Too much material around the shoulders can, however, often create a fold where the gun stock and jacket meet and so cause the gun to be incorrectly mounted.

Clothing for the moor

Nowhere are the extremes of weather more likely to be experienced than on the grouse moor. To be totally comfortable, the potential shooter requires a veritable wardrobe: an August day in North Yorkshire or Scotland can begin cold

A good saddler may be able to make up an arrangement of leather straps with which to carry one's waterproofs onto the moor

and miserable through early morning mists and drizzle, but end as a sizzling endurance test.

Because of the topography, it is often impossible to drive an all-terrain vehicle anywhere near to where the grouse are to be found and, indeed, that must be part of the sport's charm. The Guns meet at the host's house and drive as far as possible, but then everyone must leave the vehicle and walk the rest of the way. Participants in a large shoot are lucky because they can leave the carrying of guns, cartridges and shooting sticks to their loaders. Lunch is often supplied in specially constructed shooting huts or lodges and will have been brought in during the morning so that the Gun has no need to carry cumbersome packs of sandwiches. Nevertheless, the sensible shooter will wear a waxed cotton jacket and overtrousers to protect him should the weather turn rough. Waxed Egyptian cotton has certain drawbacks: when new, the material feels greasy and, in the case of overtrousers, will certainly stain the inside of a suit jacket where it comes in contact by dint of the fact that it is usually the wearer's belt which keeps the trousers in position. Waxed cotton also rubs and will wear out with continuous use as the small particles of dirt and grime act as a grinding paste on the material. On the plus side, waxed cotton does not squeak like so many other materials. It can also breathe so that the wearer does not end up as wet from his perspiration as he would had he not bothered to wear any kind of outer garment.

By its very nature, waxed material cannot be rolled into an inconspicuous parcel, so the wearer must either carry his clothes in a large game-bag or get his local saddler to make up an arrangement of thin straps which can then be hung over the shoulder. In August, a lightweight waxed cotton coat is all that is necessary. The material is usually available in two weights; the heavy-weight one will be required in October and November, which often offer the most exciting shooting. Not only is the heavier weight material waterproof but it also keeps out the bitterest wind. Unfortunately, many manufacturers skimp on the length of the coat and when leggings are worn rather than overtrousers, the effect of capillary attraction results in a wet bottom for the wearer. Ideally, one should be able to sit in the heather without the wet creeping in and a long coat means that leggings can be worn, which are infinitely more comfortable than overtrousers.

Assuming that the weather forecasters have promised a dry, sunny day for the twelfth, the grouse shooter must ensure that he is not going to be too hot and uncomfortable, especially if the estate owner expects a degree of formality from his guests – jeans, lumberjack shirts and a clay-shooting vest will not be acceptable.

In wet weather, the Gun will have no alternative but to revert to wellingtons, preferably those which are made with the sportsman in mind and, consequently, are tight fitting around the calf. If possible, you should avoid wellingtons with studded soles which have proved extremely dangerous when crossing the slippery slabs of stone in and around a moorland stream.

Woollen stockings and plus-twos prove extremely effective in protecting the legs from scratches by heather, but in warm weather it may pay to wear plus-twos made from pure cotton. Although at first touch they are of greater weight than many of the man-made lightweight versions, they are in fact much cooler. Cambrian Fly Fishers produce 'Shooting Breeks' made in either moleskin or pure cotton corduroy which are ideal for early season grouse shooting as well as looking both traditional and smart.

Boot care

Feet will become extremely hot in wellingtons or hiking boots, but ankles need some support if they are not to become twisted by walking across uneven and rocky ground. Hogg's of Fife produce an excellent variety of leather footwear, from stout shoes for the Gun to hill boots suitable for the daily wear of gamekeeper and shepherd. In order to maintain their original waterproof properties, boots need to be well cared for – although there are easier ways than the method described by Peter Hawker in his *Instructions to Young Sportsmen* (7th edition,1833):

> Take a piece of India rubber, about the size of a walnut: cut it in small pieces, and put it in a phial with four ounces of highly rectified spirits of turpentine. Cork it up for about a fortnight (more or less, according to cold or hot weather), and shake it every day. When this mixture has come to a consistency about the thickness of treacle, it is fit for use. You may then work it with a paintbrush, into leather, rope or what you please. But, when used for the soles of shoes ... or anything that does not require flexibility, you should add, to this composition, three times the amount of copal varnish. The most effectual mode of application is to anoint, not only the outside seams, but also the whole inside of the soles.
>
> If you want this dressing in a hurry, and an extra expense is no object, you will find that aether, or naphtha, will dissolve India rubber, and dry, much quicker than spirits of turpentine.

Thank heavens for the advent of dubbin!

If the weather is so warm that it becomes necessary to remove your jacket in order to shoot in comfort, the Gun who has previously been enjoying a good day's sport may find that the grouse, which up until that point had been flying directly towards his butt, suddenly veer away and provide neighbouring Guns with all the shooting. The answer to this apparent phenomenon probably lies in the colour of the Gun's shirt which, after the removal of the jacket, can be clearly seen by the birds. Remember that flankers turn the grouse by waving white flags at an opportune moment and a white or light-coloured shirt will have the same effect.

A shirt made from cotton rather than synthetic material is to be preferred for the same reasons as those described when discussing plus-twos.

Several schools of thought exist regarding the wearing of a hat on the moors. Provided that the hat is a lightweight type, it will help to protect the wearer from the sun on the hottest day and from rain dripping down his neck on the wettest. A hat with a brim will help to shield the sun from the eyes and could mean that the Gun will sight a covey of grouse sooner than he might have done otherwise. A hat also has the advantage of hiding the face, thus preventing the birds from turning. On the other hand, too wide a brim could obscure the Gun's view. If the Gun is down and out of sight behind the front wall of the butt, as he should be, he will be unseen until it is too late for the grouse to change their course even if he is hatless – provided that he does not have a bald head that shines from above.

Partridge shooting and early pheasant days

Much of what has been described as suitable apparel for the grouse moor can be worn on partridge days and early pheasant days when the weather is warm.

It is also a good idea to leave waterproof clothing in the back of a Land-Rover, so that, in the event of unexpected rain, a quick dash to the vehicle will prevent the shooter from getting too wet. You should not, however, be tempted into throwing waxproofs in a heap where they will be walked on by wet muddy dogs and wet muddy boots. Readers who have previously owned the type of coat first manufactured by Barbour will have noticed how quickly the material wears at any point where creases occur. This is not in any way the fault of the manufacturers, no matter who they are, but merely the result of continuous rubbing by miniscule particles of dirt which cling to the material because of the waterproofing substance. Dogs or unnecessary dirt will make this wear more rapid and, with this type of coat costing upwards of £100, care should be taken to make the garment last as long as possible.

Perhaps those shooters with whom I come into contact can afford the replacement. At the end of a shooting day when I chat to the Guns about their sport and place a brace of pheasants in the boot of their car, invariably I see their waterproofs thrown in and covered by boots and muddy cartridge bags and, in estate cars, providing a 'nest' for their gun-dog. This is so unnecessary: unless you are actually wearing the clothing, waterproofs should be kept neatly folded in a cheap fishing-bag or even something as simple as a plastic shopping-carrier. The whole parcel can then be transferred from car to Land-Rover and back again without damage.

There have been tremendous developments in the types of water-resistant clothing available to the Gun. Probably the most interesting is the arrival of 'Gore-Tex'. The sporting press advertises 'Gore-Tex jackets', but in actual fact there is no such thing as a Gore-Tex jacket. I believe that any material can be used provided that it sandwiches the special waterproofing substance through which the wearer's body is allowed to breathe and his perspiration escape but which still prevents any penetration by the climatic elements. Its only drawback seems to be that the favoured 'sandwiching' material tends to look like ordinary nylon and the shooter who wishes to make an impression on his friends is somewhat loath to be seen in a short jacket which looks as if it cost £20–30 from an army surplus store, whereas in fact such a garment is likely to have cost well over £100.

Pheasant days

When the weather becomes cooler, the shooter could wear as an outer garment a coat made from Loden cloth, a material which will give the reluctant Gore-Tex wearer more of a standing among his fellow Guns.

Loden is a medium-weight cloth (a mixture of pure wool and alpaca) which originates from the type of cape worn by Alpine shepherds who were known as Lodeners. The material is virtually windproof and virtually waterproof, although it becomes very heavy in persistent rain. It is a good investment for pheasant shooting.

I have on many occasions heard my beaters complain about the cold and wet weather as we line out and await the whistle to begin yet another drive, but they almost always add that they would rather be beating than standing forward shooting. Give them the opportunity and things might be different but, nevertheless, the Gun who is standing forward needs to be warm and comfortable if he is to shoot well.

Apart from wildfowling, standing at a peg while a drive is being brought in is undoubtedly one of the coldest forms of shooting and the participant must not neglect what he wears under his waterproof clothing. Standards must be maintained and the Gun who is shooting on a prestigious estate is expected to wear a traditional shooting suit.

The heaviest materials do not necessarily make for the warmest outfit and most people choose one made of Derby tweed which, because it is tightly woven, eliminates a certain loss of body heat and is not as likely to catch and tear on brambles. Most sporting outfitters can offer a range of suits or jackets and plus-twos, and it will pay the intending purchaser to look at several and try on a few before making his final choice.

It is too easy to fall into the trap of adding another layer of clothing as the weather gets colder, but with vest, shirt, waistcoat, jumper, quilted jacket, suit jacket and a Barbour, even the country's best game shots are bound to experience a frustrating day as the gun fails to mount properly, resulting in missed birds.

A T-shirt offers more warmth than a vest, and long-johns not only keep the wearer warm but also prevent any chafing of the legs in frosty weather. I have found that cotton pyjama bottoms can be worn as efficient protection from the cold and are not too bulky under plus-twos. Several thin layers of clothing are, in fact, better than, say, one thick jumper, as the warm air is trapped in small pockets between the various garments.

You should always take care to keep your feet warm and dry: once they become really cold the rest of your body soon follows suit. There are many old remedies for cold feet such as stuffing your boots with straw or wrapping newspaper around as insulation but, in my opinion, one of the best ways to ensure warm toes is to place a pair of thin socks over your woollen shooting stockings. Make sure that by doing so the fit of your feet into the boots is not restricted which will reduce circulation, causing the wearer to feel cold on even a mild day.

Boot care

Because boots take a long time to break in and become very comfortable, and also because they are, as a rule, very expensive, they deserve careful handling at the end of the day. If you do not wish to follow Peter Hawker's recipe (and not many do), the best procedure is to clean all the mud off before it dries and leave the boots where warm air can circulate around them. Under no circumstances should you try to force-dry boots by placing them next to the fire or in the airing-cupboard as this will only make the leather hard, brittle and more prone to cracking. Newspapers stuffed into boots will help absorb moisture if they are very wet and an old-fashioned pair of boot trees which you might find in an old sportsman's cupboard or at a jumble-sale will help the boots to retain their shape. Oil or dubbin should be applied when the boots are thoroughly dried (and make sure they are dry, or the oil will trap the moisture and cause it to seek a way through internally). If time permits, you should apply oil or dubbin immediately prior to another outing.

Woollen socks worn on their own tend to become full of holes in a very short space of time owing to the continual rubbing of boot or wellington; a thin pair of socks will help to prevent this and are cheaper to replace.

It is possible to buy specially designed 'welly-sox' as extra insulation, but these seem to have the disadvantage of quickly becoming sweat-ridden and, after a couple of outings, they lose their shape and size. Eventually, they slip off and make the wearer feel very uncomfortable – unless he is prepared to remove his boots continually and keep pulling the socks back into their correct position.

You can normally expect to wear wellingtons of some description at some stage during the pheasant season but, if the ground is dry or the frost is so heavy that there is the likelihood of it lasting all day, you may be able to get away with wearing the shoes worn on the grouse moor or with leather boots.

In the same sportsman's cupboard or at the same jumble-sale, you might be lucky enough to find a pair of the old-fashioned leather gaiters once favoured by farmers, keepers and shooting men alike. These have their place when combined with a good pair of leather boots and will protect the wearer from cold legs and scratches. You may receive some ribbing from fellow Guns – but what does this matter when measured against comfort?

Finally, you should always remember to take a pair of slippers to wear in the house at lunchtime. It is possible to wear the shoes in which you drove to the shoot, but slippers are probably warmer, more comfortable and give the feet a chance to return to their natural shape after being squashed into outdoor footwear all morning.

The rough shoot

The term 'rough shooting' covers a multitude of sporting activities from summer pigeon shooting over decoys to walking the hedgerows that surround a couple of horse paddocks in the hope that a rabbit or cock pheasant from the neighbouring estate may show itself. To describe one set of clothes which would be suitable for all activities would be impossible. For the sake of convenience, it is perhaps best to assume that a rough shoot contains seven or eight members who release a few hundred pheasants each year. The keepering, such as it is, is carried out by all the individuals in the syndicate and a day's bag may contain pheasants, pigeon, rabbits, ducks and an occasional partridge.

Unlike Guns standing forward all day at the driven shoot, members will probably split into two teams at the beginning of the day and each group will walk a drive and stand a drive. They will not get as cold as their counterparts and, as a result, need not worry as much about wearing warm clothing. Because they are doing more walking, however, they do need to choose a wardrobe which allows for easy movement without causing excessive perspiration.

Apart from the practicalities of plus-twos or shooting breeches and the comfort of a well-worn thornproof jacket, for the sake of tradition and creating a neat and tidy impression to other country users, it is a good idea to dress correctly for the occasion even when lunch consists only of sandwiches eaten in the barn rather than served by house staff in the host's dining-room.

The rough shooter will find the wearing of thornproof, waterproof leggings to his advantage even when there is not the slightest likelihood of rain. Leggings will protect his legs as he beats through the brambles, they will prevent him from becoming drenched as he splashes through the muddy gateway used twice daily by the milking herd, and, by keeping his knees dry, they will fend off rheumatism in later years. There will be many occasions when he needs to kneel – tying up birds, for instance, or dropping down out of sight of a passing flock of pigeons or pack of mallard. With such rough wear, clothes will not last as long as they would with careful treatment and, for this reason (as well as because they are more comfortable), it is advisable to buy leggings that are cheaper to replace.

If you do not have a tweed jacket, an army surplus jumper or a quilted shooter's waistcoat are ideal when worn under a waxed coat, but you should bear in mind that too much bulk will cause faults to develop when the gun is brought to the shoulder. This is especially important in rough shooting, when the quarry is more likely to rise unexpectedly and demand some quick snap shooting.

A hat is useful for any type of shooting, but on the rough shoot it can also prove an effective aid in camouflaging the wearer from an incoming pigeon or wildfowl. On cold days, a hat also protects the wearer against heat loss via the head (medically accepted as being an appreciable source of heat loss). You should choose a hat which stays in place no matter what the angle of the head, and make sure that it will protect your eyes, especially if you wear glasses. A wide brim will also prevent rain from dripping down your neck, although to be absolutely certain of eradicating this nuisance it is best to wear a towelling cravat which will absorb any wet before it trickles on to your shirt and makes life uncomfortable. Alternatively, a small hand-towel or tea-towel kept in the poacher's pocket is also effective for mopping up water, but it has the disadvantage of being somewhat cumbersome around the neck – so this is a rare instance where a purpose-designed item proves to be a good investment.

In my own pocket I keep such a cravat bought several years ago for a few pence and a flat cap made from waxproof material. The only problem occurs when I leave my coat in the cab of the tractor which is pulling the beater's trailer and find myself without any form of protection during an unexpected shower of rain or snow.

The wildfowler

The true wildfowler is so hardened that I hesitate to recommend any suitable clothing for him. If you read some of the old accounts of punt gunning and mornings by the foreshore written by such guns as Abe Chapman, it is easy to forget just how much of an ordeal such shooting can be. To sit silently and still until your balaclava freezes over and the dog's coat becomes covered with tiny icicles is an unknown experience for me and one, I must admit, that I am not keen to try.

Briefly, then, the clothes of a wildfowler are in a class of their own. Arran sweaters (naturally oil impregnated), thermal underwear and waders are a necessity, as are the heaviest type of waxed coat and overtrousers. A knitted woollen balaclava appears to be the favourite headwear which protects head, ears and mouth from the worst of the weather.

The wildfowler's dog also needs to be 'clad' agains the weather, but it does not require a special coat of the type seen on poodles and terriers along city streets. Two hessian sacks are all that are necessary: one on which the dog can sit to protect his nether regions from the cold ground and the other laid across his back, which not only prevents the effects of frost from penetrating the animal's body, but also gives a light-coloured dog some form of camouflage.

Summer shooting

Camouflage seems to be the priority subject in any discussion of summer shooting. The type of shooting which springs immediately to mind is pigeon shooting over decoys and, to be successful at this, it is important that you blend in with the surroundings.

As most of this kind of shooting is done from a hide, a lightweight camouflage suit is probably the ideal apparel as it breaks up the shooter's silhouette against a natural background. With luck, the weather which has allowed harvesting to take place will remain set fair for the pigeon shooter as he sets his decoys out on the stubble and he need wear only a shirt (dark, of course) under his camouflage jacket. Ordinary shoes or trainers will be sufficient to protect his feet from thorns or brambles and allow them to breathe.

Some estates hold vermin shoots in the spring or early summer and Guns and beaters who have kept in contact during the close season will often be invited to take part. As jays, magpies and foxes will be the most likely quarry, it is important to use some form of discreet clothing. It is not necessary to go to the trouble of purchasing army clothes. Dark colours will suffice and it is more important to position yourself in the correct place and merge into your surroundings than it is to wear the right garments.

Clothing conclusions

Clothing for any sport should allow freedom of movement; it should not be so loud as to stand out, and it should be warm without proving cumbersome.

You should look for the ideal garment to meet individual needs, then buy the best that you can afford. Too many shooters make the mistake of buying every piece of clothing on offer at the Game Fair or local country show. They then wear them once, find them unsuitable and relegate them to a cupboard – and they still shiver or get drenched when actually shooting.

4
Guns, Keepers and the Shooting Day

The shooting day itself contains much to bewilder the inexperienced Gun. Although the invited or paying guest needs only to concentrate on shooting game and not his fellow Gun, he will miss much of the enjoyment the day has to offer if he cannot, or will not, try to understand what is happening and how events are organised.

It is a constant complaint among experienced sportsmen that too many inexperienced people on 'company shoots' do not understand that they have obligations not only to their host but also to the owner of the shoot if he is not the host, to the keeper, to the beaters and to the other guests.

Experienced sportsmen worry, too, about the apparent disregard for gun safety and bemoan the fact that the days have gone when young shots spent many days with their father or his keeper just watching and being instructed before they were allowed to take an unloaded gun on a shoot, when they were expected to follow all the procedures until the tutor was certain that no lapse of safety would occur, however exciting the moment.

Dress, too, is criticised. One knowledgeable person I know

who was brought up well versed in the old traditions and who has now given up his own shooting so that a neighbouring estate can take advantage of his acres, for which he receives in return at least five days' sport, remarked that the majority of his fellow Guns could not be experienced because their clothes were incorrect.

Undoubtedly, dress is indicative of the man, especially if everything is new. What worried this particular Gun most of all, however, was the amount of entertaining that took place: drinks on arrival, hip flasks, pre-prandial refreshment and yet more socialising at the end of the day – these were not his idea of a good shoot. Although not strictly relevant to this chapter, it is nevertheless worth commenting on the fact that alcohol and guns are a potentially deadly combination and shoot organisers could do well to restrict the levels of entertaining that take place.

Christian name or surname?

It is usually only on the old inherited estates where the keeper is late middle-aged and his father was keeper before him that the owner and his guests continue to call him by his surname. The casual Gun should not, therefore, call any of the keepers by their surname. If you have not been able to find out the keeper's Christian name, it is preferable to say 'Hey, keeper'. No other trade or walk of life suffers from the 'surname syndrome' like shooting does and the sooner it is eradicated, the better. If the keeper is fully acquainted with all aspects of his employment, the use of a Christian name will not encourage familiarity and although I have known several keepers who call their employers by their first names when on their own, they had no problem on a shooting day in using the prefix 'Mr' or 'Sir'.

The first thing the newcomer should do (after he has dragged his new Barbour through the mud in an effort to age it!) is to acquaint himself fully with the layout of the estate and to try to work out from the positioning of the gun pegs how and why the woods are being driven.

If he is likely to be shooting there again, it would be a good idea to learn the names of the coverts. Even if he will not be shooting there again, the name of the keeper and his key helpers can soon be learned. Their impressions of a person can be mellowed with kindly treatment and, at the end of the day, they will pass a comment among themselves like, 'The chap on number 4 peg at West Wood couldn't hit a barn door but he's a good bloke, said hello and gave me a sip from his flask,' rather than a remark such as 'That chap on number 4 might as well have stayed at home – couldn't shoot and was a right arrogant so-and-so – think he thought he owned the place.'

On the day of the shoot itself, the keeper will have greater problems than who calls him what. In the keeper's eyes, all the Gun has to do is to turn up on the right day and with the right equipment and clothing. The keeper, on the other hand, has his beaters to employ and organise, gun pegs to situate, 'stops', pickers-up and the game-cart driver who all need special instructions if they are to carry out their jobs without having to run back constantly to him to ask what to do next.

To the Guns and beaters, a shooting day is a day of enjoyment and relaxation, but to the keeper it is his employment. On shoots where only seven or eight days are planned, the gamekeeper is put into the situation of having only a week to show what he has been doing for the other fifty-one. No wonder, then, that the keeper can appear to be a little preoccupied, to say the least, if you happen to catch sight of him on his way to the first drive.

If you are shooting for the first time, it is a safe assumption that the chosen quarry will be pheasants. They are, after all the easiest to rear and stock in large numbers and will adapt to most of the environmental situations that this country offers.

Driven pheasant days

By whatever means you have achieved access to a day's shooting, the procedures upon reaching the venue remain basically the same.

Apart from showing good manners, it will pay the individual Gun to arrive in plenty of time. Although the day is intended to be one of enjoyment, any new Gun is bound to feel a little apprehensive and nervous and, as he climbs into his transport vehicle, will undoubtedly worry that he has forgotten something and be checking his pocket or bag for cartridges, making sure that it is his gun in the cover and not someone else's in a similar case, or that his waterproofs are tucked under the spare wheel and not left in a bag by the back wheel of his car. By arriving in plenty of time, he has every opportunity to double-check his equipment as well as getting to know fellow guests who will undoubtedly be feeling equally apprehensive.

When all the guests have arrived, the host will bring round his leather wallet containing the gun-peg numbers. As explained elsewhere, the process should ensure that each Gun stands at least one chance during the day of getting a good peg. Make sure that you are not the one who forgets your number by the second drive and has to admit to your neighbour that you are not sure where you are supposed to be.

It is a pleasant experience for the Gun to stand at his peg and absorb his surroundings, especially in the early part of the season when the woods are still full of autumn colour, but he should also use the time to calculate how the drive is being driven. This is not always as simple as it may seem and even the positioning of the gun pegs can leave the Gun wondering which way he should be facing. This dilemma usually occurs when a ride has been cut through a wooded area so that the covert can be driven from west to east and then east to west, necessitating two sets of pegs. Most keepers in this situation try to point the relevant pegs in the direction of on-coming birds. On some drives, it may be possible for the keeper and his employer to peg out two entirely different stands to accommodate any unfavourable wind directions on the shooting day itself. Such drives are, unfortunately, in the minority and the shoot may either have to substitute a drive completely or move the Guns around when birds refuse to co-operate because the wind is too strong. These last-minute changes are the concern of the host and his keeper and the guests must abide by their decision.

Stops and stopping

A 'stop' needs to be sensible and reliable for he has to work on his own initiative for most of the day. The end of the drive is his domain and, if he does his job correctly, he could be the deciding factor in the successful shoot.

Most keepers will choose an older member of the team for stop's duties because people in this age group have probably seen the best of traditional pheasant shooting as boys, before progressing to become reliable members of the estate's team of beaters. When, in later age, they can no longer walk the full distance, they prove very useful in knowing exactly what the keeper is trying to achieve.

While loading for different people, I have heard them comment, sometimes derogatorily, on the actions of a stop. The stop always acts with the shoot's best interests at heart and if he suddenly taps his stick against a tree when it seems to the Gun that he has prevented pheasants from flying over his head, there will have been a very good reason and the remainder of the drive will benefit from his actions.

The stop has other uses. Many estates now use CB radios or walkie-talkies to keep shooters and beaters in touch. The stop, therefore, can inform the keeper when the Guns are in position or tell him that only the pegs on the left are getting any shooting and the keeper should perhaps push his left-hand beaters further forward in order to give the right-hand side some sport. Where it is necessary to use more than one person as a stop, a small group can blank in a hedgerow or rough piece of ground in order to push a few straying birds into the drive.

The stop does not always remain on the outer perimeter of the coverts and some drives need the addition of sewelling to help encourage pheasants to fly. Sewelling is often more effective when someone is making it move.

Sewelling consists of thin strips of white plastic strung in a line about 54ft (50m) from the end of the drive. The purpose of sewelling is that it should be positioned across an open ride to encourage birds to fly to their best advantage. The Game Conservancy have, during their many years of research into the habits of pheasants, found that in order to fly well, birds need to take off in a well-cleared area so that, if one were to draw an imaginary trajectory from take-off to gun-line, the ideal position would be at an angle of about 30°. If it is any less, the bird will be exhausted from the effort of take-off; any more, and it will begin to drop and will not be worth a shot. Provided that the sewelling is correctly positioned, this should be no problem, especially when a stop is positioned to agitate the string and frighten the quarry into flying.

Pickers-up

Pickers-up need to be considered throughout the day if accidents are to be avoided. They can only do their job effectively when they are positioned immediately behind the line; they will make every attempt to be as unobtrusive as possible, but they need to stand where they and their dogs can get a good view of dead or, more importantly, wounded birds.

If you take a bird behind when it is dropping into cover, it is all too easy to hit one of the pickers-up and, because of the nature of low-ground shooting, they will undoubtedly be within shotgun range when an injury could prove fatal. Pickers-up are less vulnerable on the grouse moors and partridge manors, where it is more usual for pickers-up to be stationed at least 100 yd (91m) behind the Guns.

> **Pickers-up** are present to make sure that no wounded game is left, so it would be foolish to approach a picker-up at the end of the drive and tell him that a certain number of birds are still lying on the ground when he will have been keeping an exact record of how many birds have fallen.

A few years ago, I was loading for a very experienced Gun on a large and famous shoot, when a woodcock flew out in front of us. As the beaters were in sight, it was impossible for him to shoot forward, so he turned and took the bird behind. As he changed guns, he remarked to me, ‘Oh, that was a bit low, wasn’t it? I hope there were no pickers-up there.’ Had there been, such hopes would have arrived too late and, at that range, an injury might have occurred.

There is so much to think about before squeezing the trigger, but it is much better to be known as a safe shot who is unable to hit anything rather than as an excellent shot who is careless about where he points his gun. If only such a Gun could see the fights which ensue among the beaters as they come to the end of the drive and realise that they are the ones immediately in front of such a cowboy, it would probably shame him into better behaviour.

Throughout the drive, you should keep a careful check on how many birds are down and dead and in what direction they have fallen. Marking like this is much easier on the pheasant drive than it is on the vast acres of open moorland. There is always an individual tree or a fence whereby you can count the number of posts from the left in order to remind yourself where a certain bird has fallen on the pheasant shoot. Grouse shooters need to devise their own methods and one person for whom I loaded when I was employed as a moor keeper used to position spent cartridges in the general direction of each bird down. Thus, he was not only able to see the direction and remind himself of the distance out from the butt, but could also tell the pickers-up exactly how many grouse were shot. Although I loaded for him only once, his previous record on that moor was so good that the experienced pickers-up knew that what he said was the truth: if he said he had two birds in a direct line to the peat gulley, they had only to work their dogs in that direction to pick them up without difficulty.

Having picked up myself, I know that there are Guns who wrongly convince themselves and others about their prowess with a shotgun. At the end of a drive, they can be seen rushing about picking their neighbours' birds in order to add them to their pile at the base of the gun peg. This behaviour is of no use to the pickers-up; they need to know exactly what is down and are not impressed to be sent off several fields away in search of a pricked pheasant only to put the dogs forward and find the suspect bird fly away as unharmed as the day it was hatched.

The keeper informs his pickers-up which drives are to be included in the day's shooting and they know exactly what to expect. With three or four pickers-up on the payroll, they are able to decide among themselves who is covering what Gun. As the average shoot invites only eight guests, this leaves one picker-up per two Guns. For pickers-up with experience and a couple of good dogs, this causes no problems and the casual shooter need not worry about their activities provided that he remembers that they are, in fact, there.

Beaters and the beating line

Members of the beating line are no longer recruited from the estate workforce. In these days of economy and more automated farming methods, family retainers are no longer relied upon. Some of the larger estates may be more fortunate and could make use of woodsmen and foresters, but it is more likely that you will find the only farming member of the team pressed into service driving the beaters' trailer.

Instead, today's beaters come from all walks of life. In my current team I have site agents, car mechanics, service managers, carpenters, British Telecom engineers and electricity linesmen. When numbers are down, an accountant can be called upon to help out. Bearing in mind that the latter could expect to earn about £50 an hour by sitting in his office and only £13 a day by beating, it is obviously not money which attracts a ready supply of beaters. Without exception, they have an interest in shooting, either at clays or rearing birds for their own small shoot or just watching others enjoy themselves. Some beaters may have a working gun-dog which they have spent many hours training and wish to see how it behaves before entering it for a field trial, or perhaps they intend to use it just to help flush out a few extra birds.

No matter where these people beat, they would, I am sure, participate in a shoot to enjoy a day in the countryside – knowing that they will be among friends – without any form of remuneration being offered. A payment is made, however, and this probably pays for their petrol and perhaps half a bottle of spirit with which to fill their hip flask.

Remember then, as a Gun, that you should never fall into the trap of feeling that the beaters are somehow inferior to you. On one occasion, for example, a guest had treated a particular beater with some contempt. A few days later they met again, but this time the beater was sitting behind the bank manager's desk and the Gun, full of embarrassment, was asking for a business loan!

A good keeper will also be good at man management and should be able to get his team to beat efficiently even when the ground is steep and the going is difficult. No brambles will be impenetratable to the really enthusiastic beater who is enjoying the day but, to be sure of helpers of this calibre, the keeper needs to inform everyone of their particular duties.

Whenever time allows, the keeper will have told the beaters what drives are on the list for the day. If an old-established covert is being experimented with and taken in a completely new direction, there will usually be plenty of opportunity for the keeper to gather his beaters together while the Guns get into position, and tell them exactly what the day's plans are.

The new beater requires some extra attention from the keeper if he is to fit in and enjoy himself. It is not always possible to be precise, but it could save a loss of temper a few minutes later if the person in charge of the line could tell the newcomer, 'We are heading for that row of oaks, but let the left hand come on before setting off.'

Generally, the beaters will line out an equal distance apart at the end of a wood or game-cover crop and, on a given signal (usually a whistle from the keeper or a shot fired in the air from the host), proceed steadily and quietly towards the line of waiting Guns.

If beaters are thin on the ground, it may be necessary for them to zigzag about in order to tap out all available cover, thus creating some wide gaps through which birds can either run or fly back and escape.

If a straight line were kept on every drive, birds could also break out on either side of the cover before reaching the Guns, so a competent beating team will push forward on either the right or left when this happens. Very often, the beaters have to act on their own initiative: pheasants could escape unnecessarily if the beaters waited for several minutes while they sought approval for their actions from the keeper, who is normally in the middle of the line.

On some drives, previous experience may have proved that the only way to drive the birds successfully is to form the line into a horseshoe shape before the signal to start is given. Other drives may be so large that it is necessary to split the beaters into two or three groups, each bringing in a separate section until, at a certain point, the line joins together for the final 100yd (91m). If one group pushes forward too eagerly, birds could be missed by the other two teams because, after a few shooting days, game soon becomes adept at looking for any quiet places and escaping through them.

Most keepers and shoot owners prefer a quiet team of beaters, but there are two very distinct schools of thought on this. On the one hand, there are those who feel that a great deal of vocal noise encourages birds to rise and fly throughout the drive rather than running right to the sewelling before they flush in one large pack. Others believe that not only is just the rhythmic sound of sticks tapping the trees more pleasing, but also pheasants will run forward and not flush until it is too late for them to fly without going over the gun line.

Under no circumstances should a Gun attempt to interfere with the beating line, except, perhaps, to inform an outside beater that birds are running out just out of his sight. This may be expected and a stop might already be in position who has not been noticed by the Gun. Even when the owner of a shoot calls out to the beaters to 'hold the left hand' or to 'push on the left hand', generally the majority will ignore his remarks and listen instead to the keeper's instructions. In such a situation, however, the keeper cannot win and if his beaters do obey the employer's commands and stop, the pheasants will run back through the gap that has been created. If the beaters ignore the host and things still go wrong, the keeper will be chastised for disobedience.

The sensible keeper will carefully vet any beater who asks to bring his dog. Most dogs will be trained and capable of being stopped when birds begin to flush, but it only needs a lapse on the part of the handler or an unexpected rabbit to bolt to cause a dog to run forward and flush all the pheasants which have been carefully pushed towards the end of the drive – an action that is unlikely to endear either dog or owner to anyone. On the other hand, Guns must appreciate the fact that, without a few dogs in the line, many birds would be left behind and for this reason alone perhaps the Gun would do well to turn a blind eye occasionally when someone's dog momentarily goes out of control. The handler will feel uncomfortable enough without any further comments being necessary.

A good team of beaters will know the importance of keeping a straight line and they should also know when to stop as the birds begin to fly. By doing so, they should prevent any great flushes and give the Guns a chance to reload after taking a shot.

Finally, it is worth pointing out that, no matter how far the beaters have to travel between drives, they always seem to be ready and in position long before the Guns, even when the latter need only to turn round and change numbers. With a little more speed and effort on the part of the Guns, it might be possible to fit in an extra drive and, instead of the seven or eight drives normally carried out by most shoots, perhaps even an unscheduled duck flight could be added.

End-of-season 'excess'

It is interesting to note that the beaters, when they hold their end-of-season 'cock day', will manage to fit in at least a dozen drives before it is time to retire to the keeper's cottage to discuss the season's events over a glass or two of whisky.

Flagmen

Although I personally loathe the idea, it seems to be becoming increasingly popular on some shoots to station a couple of beaters between the end of the drive and the gun line. Armed with flags, they are expected to wave them frantically whenever birds approach in an effort to make them fly higher. In an ideal world, drives from which pheasants will not fly high and sportingly without such artificial aids would not be included in the day's itinerary, but it must be admitted that few estates are in the fortunate position of having so many drives that certain woods can be left undisturbed throughout the season.

Before resorting to flagmen, these shoots should experiment with every possible way of driving the covert. All too often you hear the keeper or his employer damn a new idea because 'it's always been driven this way and I remember father having some great shooting at this peg twenty years ago'. A great deal can happen in twenty years and a wood which was young then and from which game showed itself to its best advantage may now be too thick and the trees too tall for a pheasant to be able to fly forward. There is nothing to be lost by experimenting after Christmas when birds are thinner on the ground and little is at stake.

If all else fails, there may be no alternative but to stand flagmen forward, but it should be done in such a way that the standing Guns do not feel hindered by their presence. Too enthusiastic a flagman, however, may have the effect of turning birds away from the line, leaving the Guns frustrated.

After condemning them out of hand, there is one situation where flagmen could prove useful and that is if they are positioned on the outer flanks of the beating line or as a continuation of the gun line. Placed thus, it is just possible that they might succeed in turning birds towards the Guns which would otherwise break out from the sides. There is, then, more skill and knowledge involved in being a flagman whose duties are similar to those of the flanker's for grouse and partridge driving.

Loaders and loading

If you are very fortunate, you may be lucky enough to be invited to a shoot on a day when double guns are used. Many agencies also offer some sport for which the Gun has the opportunity to bring along two weapons.

The first problem you are likely to encounter is to find a pair of matched guns. Although it may be possible to borrow a gun from a friend to match your own, it will not be the same weight for weight, so the shooting performance is bound to suffer. Needless to say, a pair (whether matched or not) should at least be both side-by-sides or both over-and-unders and not a combination of the two. Ridiculous though this remark may sound, I was once asked to load for an individual in an American party and, upon reaching the first drive and getting the guns out of the slips, I found that he had indeed brought a combination of guns with him.

Upon reaching the gun peg, it is worth having a few practice runs and passing the guns to the loader and back again. With weapons being so expensive, it pays not to drop them too often.

If the Gun shoots from his right shoulder, it is normal for the loader to stand on his right, a pace or two back to

Gun hire costs

It is now possible to hire a pair of top-class English guns from about £60 for a weekend. A gun for a week will cost about £95, plus a further £55 for each subsequent week. Perhaps this is an alternative for the casual Gun who does not wish to invest about £18,500 for a basic Purdey side-lock or £23,500 for an over-and-under, where prices rocket because of the more complicated mechanism.

'It is now possible to hire a pair of top-class English guns . . .' This engraving, taken from the side plates of a Holland & Holland, shows some of the incredible craftsmanship and skill taken in their construction

avoid interfering with his swing. Provided that the loader is competent, his natural reflexes should be enough to save him from being hit on the head by the gun barrels and the shooter should be able to swing around as freely as if he were alone. It helps, however, if the loader is approximately the same height as the Gun.

When you change one weapon for another, it is normal for the barrels to be held straight up in the air after firing. The Gun will by then have the empty weapon in his right hand and, by pivoting the upper half of his body, it should be possible for him to reach out towards the loader for the new gun without taking his eyes from the direction of the drive. The gun will be given to him across the palm of his outstretched left hand and, at the same time, the loader will use his own left hand to relieve the Gun of the empty weapon. Many who are experienced with double-gun shooting insist that the loader actually and quite forcibly slaps the loaded gun hard into the left hand, the action helping the shooter to take an immediate and strong grip.

For the person who is more used to shooting with a single gun, it can be difficult to remember not to break the weapon as if he were going to reload it himself. This spoils the system completely and could result in dropped guns or, at the very least, the crashing of barrels.

You should not expect the loader to be able to mark and count the number of birds that are down. His job is difficult enough – pulling cartridges from the bag, ducking and weaving and, if the Gun is accompanied by a companion, remembering to eject the cartridges in a direction where they will not hit the friend.

When things go well and a good team is created, there is much pleasure to be had in the relationship by both the shooter and his loader. If both have coped admirably with a flush or two, a little mutual admiration will help to cement the relationship.

Because such teamwork is so important, many Guns insist on taking along their own loader. If it is impossible to find someone with the small amount of knowledge necessary for safe gun handling, however, the shoot will undoubtedly be able to supply one. On a commercial shoot, a charge may be made for such services, but normally the loader is tipped at the end of the day. The amount of the tip varies from shoot to shoot and is something to be discussed with the host.

I know of someone who was fortunate enough to be asked to load for an Arab guest who, during the course of casual conversation, happened to tell his loader what he made financially in business throughout the year. At the end of the day the Arab pressed six £10 notes into his loader's hands (this was at a time when just one £10 note would have been more than fair payment) and the loader, once he returned home, worked out that it had taken longer for the Gun to take the money from his pocket and give it to him than it had for his business interests to acquire it!

Partridge shooting

> Happy the man, no doubt, who lived in those days when the hand-reaped stubble was knee-deep, and the pointer beat the field for him with mathematical precision. He could go out any fine afternoon, accompanied only by a keeper with a bag, and return in a couple of hours with eight to ten brace of partridges and an appetite. But for us no such joy remains. The stubbles are as close shaven as a monk's pate. The pointer's occupation is gone, and to the spaniel, the straight, narrow, knife-like ridges of economical modern fences afford no opportunities for research or discovery. We must make a business of our sport and systematically organise the day's proceedings. We can do no good alone. We must have two or three shooters at least, and the game walked up by or driven to the dogless sportsmen.

The above was not, as might at first be imagined, written by a sportsman of the 1980s bemoaning and regretting the type of partridge shooting which his grandfather must have enjoyed, but was penned by W. Bromley-Davenport in the 'new' edition of his book *Sport*, which was published in 1888. It would appear from this that partridge shooting has been in decline for many years, but it did, in fact, undergo a revival at the beginning of this century. The methods were different then and those 'two or three shooters' increased to a team of seven or eight who relied upon beaters to find them their sport. With competent keepers, partridge manors could be guaranteed good bags of English partridges.

Nowadays, the new shooter will be very lucky if he receives an invitation on a formal partridge day. The most that the average Gun can reasonably expect is for a few French partridges to be released in the game covers in the hope that they will be encouraged to fly and thus provide a minor diversion on a pheasant day. As such, the partridges will not be worthy of special treatment by the keeper or his beaters.

On days when partridges are the sole intended quarry, well-qualified beaters are probably the most important factor. Obviously, fields rather than woods are being driven and the straight line previously discussed with regard to pheasants will be changed for one in which the beaters are required to create a horseshoe-shaped line and wave flags across the stubble in the hope of getting a covey of birds to fly towards the standing Guns. There is skill in such work and the words of Charles Alington in 1904 in his book entitled *Partridge Driving* serve just as well today:

> The great art of driving consists in showing as many beaters to the birds as possible when they first rise, before they have had time to decide on a line of flight for themselves. Flags should therefore only be used by beaters who are out of sight themselves when the rest of the line is in full view of the birds . . . Flanking in an undulating country is more than half the battle, and the attempt to get it done properly is often heart-breaking work. The arrival of the man with the flag at a given spot a second too soon or too late will make all the difference to the success or failure of the drive.'

Pickers-up will stand further back than they would on a pheasant day because of the layout of the land, and the dog's chief qualities should be threefold: 'He must have pace, a good nose, and high courage ... A tender mouth might be added.'

Where an attempt at partridge driving proper is made, the guns may be positioned behind a hedge over which birds are expected to fly or, on exceptionally open farmland, hessian rides or straw bales may be specially built. Probably the most famous partridge manor in England is that at Six Mile Bottom and anyone who has driven past the estate cannot help but notice how the hedgerows have been cut to accommodate both Gun and loader.

Dangerous shooting

The greatest problem on a partridge shoot concerns dangerous shooting. With large, open expanses which give no real indication of distances, there is always difficulty in gauging when a bird is within shot and just how far the pellets will travel if a miss occurs and there are no trees or undergrowth to 'catch' the shot. The low flight of partridge, whether they be English or French, adds to the possible dangers and it is much easier to 'pepper' pickers-up or beaters accidentally – a point of which the Gun must be constantly aware.

Grouse shooting

A totally different day's shooting is in the offing if you accept an invitation to the grouse moor, although the safety problems which concern the partridge shooter apply equally to the person who chooses to shoot grouse.

Again, it can be difficult to assess the amount of time which one has upon seeing the first covey of birds heading towards the butts. To shoot too soon means a pricked or missed grouse; to shoot too late (always supposing that one connects) results in a bird suitable only for grouse fricassée.

Undulations in the topography may mean that the Gun could be looking forward and seeing no sign of the beaters one minute, but the next he may see them appearing over the brow of the hill, well within shot.

All the beaters should carry flags with which to encourage the grouse to fly forward and not back over their heads.

Flankers

Unlike the flagmen on a pheasant drive who are positioned in front of the gun line in an effort to make poor flyers present some sort of sporting shot, flankers on the grouse moor are positioned several hundred yards from the end butts to turn grouse towards the waiting guns.

Although to the inexperienced shooter, the flankers (usually neighbouring keepers) generally seem to be taking life easy, lying back in the heather and enjoying the August sunshine, they are an important part of the day's sport. Their duties, however, are not always fully understood.

It is essential that flankers keep out of sight until the last possible moment. From his reclined position, the flanker can see the oncoming birds, assess their probable flight line and, if they look to be a little wide, jump up from his hiding place and wave the flag. It is the element of surprise which is likely to turn the birds rather than just an erratic use of a flag. So, the man with the flag must not be afraid to use his own initiative and, in order to achieve the best possible results, he must know the ground and the line most likely to be taken by grouse under the various weather and wind conditions (hence the reason that most moor keepers use their neighbouring colleagues).

In some situations it may be necessary for all the flankers to position themselves on one side of the butts, about 75yd (68m) apart and at an angle of about 45° from the end gun. Normally, however, a team will be expected to cover both sides, although a third alternative may be necessary if a drive is being taken along the side of a hill when the keeper will find it useful to stock the topside with flagmen because grouse are inclined to follow the higher contours.

The other major difference on the grouse moor is the number of drives which can be fitted into the day. Because of the vast number of acres available for sport, it is unlikely that the grouse shooter will have the chance to change his peg number more than four times, unlike those on the pheasant shoot who could expect to enjoy seven or eight drives in the day.

Transport from drive to drive

The pheasant or partridge shoot is likely to be more fortunate than the grouse moor in being able to supply transport for the Guns to ease their journey from drive to drive. Some of the more remote moors have terrain which is impassable even in the best four-wheel-drive vehicle, but once the venue for the first drive has been reached, it is often only necessary for the individual to walk a few hundred yards to reach the butts for each subsequent beat.

On an estate where pheasants are the main objective, it is important for the Guns to be fully mobile if they are not to waste valuable time travelling from drive to drive. Transport will also help to outwit some wary pheasants towards the end of the season and, by being able to move quickly, it should be possible to bring in one drive at one end of the estate before moving towards the other boundary and doing the same there. In this way, those suspicious cock birds who seem very adept at rushing down the nearest hedgerow at the first sign of danger can often be prevented from doing so because of the element of surprise.

A few points should be considered when using the various forms of transport. The casual Gun who has just taken possession of his first ever four-wheel-drive vehicle is often keen to volunteer his machine's services in the convoy purely out of a desire to put the vehicle through its paces. Without some knowledge of driving through mud and unfamiliar terrain, it is all too easy for the inexperienced driver to get bogged down and thus delay the day's proceedings by necessitating fellow Guns to push and pull him out of trouble. This in itself causes disturbance to the next drive, especially when all the participants of the rescue party have imbibed a little too freely from their hip flasks and bottles of sloe gin and tend to be a little vocal.

Noise problems

Any shouting, horn blasting and door slamming is to be discouraged. I have seen such an incident occur when all the birds which were already near the flushing ride ran back as far as the stops would allow them, before taking off and flying back over the heads of the beaters. The host then proceeded to blame the keeper for driving the woods wrongly!

It is, therefore, advantageous to transport the Guns en masse in a horse-box type of trailer pulled by a tractor. In this way everyone remains together, there is very little door slamming (especially when the tailgate has been removed), participants remain dry, and their cartridges, wet-weather clothing and any refreshments are all under one roof. Another benefit is that a tractor driver, who can move the transport to wherever it is wanted next, will probably be employed rather than one of the four-wheel-drive owners having to rush back and pick up his vehicle at the end of the drive.

Camouflage

A tractor and trailer are easier to park out of sight than is a row of motors which may be many coloured and have been known to deter pheasants from flying forward.

The game-cart driver, if there is one, or the pickers-up if there is not, will be responsible for the care of any shot birds, so it should not be necessary for the Guns to burden either their trailer or their own vehicles with dead game. Most shoots prefer the Guns to leave the birds at the base of the peg from which point they will be collected, counted and hung on rails to cool off properly. There is nothing more infuriating to the keeper who tallies up the score at the end of the day and reports the total bag to the shooters, only to be asked, 'Oh, does that include the two brace in the spare wheel of my Land-Rover?' Apart from confusing the keeper, the birds themselves will probably be in less than pristine condition in such circumstances, especially on a wet or muddy day.

At the end of the day

At the end of the shooting day, whether it be one pursuing grouse, pheasant or partridge or an informal day pursuing a few pigeons, the emphasis should be on thanking one's host for an enjoyable time. (In the case of a pigeon shoot, a brief visit to the farmhouse in order to offer thanks and perhaps part of the bag will help to ensure that further visits are welcomed.)

Even when the Gun is participating in a purely commercial venture, etiquette is still very important and a happy send-off sets the seal on a perfect day. For those Guns who have travelled a long distance, a substantial tea may be in order. Others may wish to make an immediate start on their homeward journey, so they should not be kept waiting for the brace of birds traditionally given to each Gun by the shoot.

Personally, I try to sort out these birds at lunchtime, thus making sure that the game is both cool and dry. The game-cart driver should have his totals sorted out by the start of the last drive so that his only remaining job when that drive is finished is to add the numbers to his previously calculated bag. I can then be at the front door of the house at the same time as the Guns are changing their boots for some more suitable footwear – a fact which they seem to appreciate. On other shoots I have seen an otherwise well-organised day collapse at this juncture, with the keeper (and sometimes the host as well) disappearing for what seems like hours on end to count and sort out the final bag. This often leaves the guests waiting, especially on a commercial shoot when the individual is not necessarily among friends and is unsure of what to do next.

The subject of tipping the keeper has been discussed in Chapter 1, but perhaps it should be pointed out that a few comments on a particularly enjoyable drive will never go amiss, while a drive which has gone obviously wrong should never be commented on. The keeper, of all people, will be well aware of any disasters and it is sure to be a subject for further conversation at a later date if the host was also disappointed.

Looking after one's gun

There is a saying in the hunting world that the sportsman should see to his horse before seeing to himself. This saying has broadened into any aspect of field sports and been used to impress upon the gun-dog owner the importance of attending to the comfort of his dog before going into the house, bathing, changing and enjoying a large whisky. The gun, although an inanimate object, needs as much attention as an animal, especially if you are lucky enough to own a good quality weapon which will appreciate in value.

Because of their rarity, guns such as those made by Purdey's, Holland & Holland and Boss have proved to be a good investment over the years and there has been considerable rise in demand and prices during the past five years. Such guns, therefore, deserve the best of attention and it is important that they travel from shoot to shoot in sound, well-fitting, box-type cases. (It is equally important that, during the shoot, they should be carefully sleeved between drives to minimise damage.)

On a day when loaders are employed, they will clean and store the gun and, being keepers or others who understand the gun's working mechanisms, they will ensure that the weapon will be suitably cared for in readiness for its next outing.

Those less fortunate on a single gun day should never lean their guns against a wall, on the top of a car bonnet or against the side of a vehicle. I once saw the owner of a Land-Rover who had lent his motor on a grouse shoot, drive off to see to his sheep stocks and run over a very expensive pair of guns because they had been leant against the vehicle while their owner changed into something more comfortable. Both butts were broken and the owner's future insurance premiums were most likely increased.

Gun care

Before storing the gun between outings, first make certain that it is absolutely clean and dry. The barrels are probably the most vulnerable to corrosion and special care must be taken to ensure that all traces of leading are removed from the bores. Attention should also be given to the sides of the ribs as it is all too easy for grit and moisture to collect in the rib channels. There are plenty of good brands of gun grease on the market and this should be used to cover the barrels lightly, inside and out; the action should be covered in a similar way.

The stock and fore-end are easier to deal with. A toothbrush can be used to clear the chequering of mud before a good wood preservative is applied. If the gun is to be used again in the near future, a wipe with an oily rag is probably sufficient for 'lock, stock and barrel'. In any event, a slightly oily rag should never touch the weapon: any hand-touch on the metal will undoubtedly result in rusty fingerprint marks within a matter of hours.

The quality of the gun sleeve is important and obviously

a thin sleeve offers less protection against mishaps than a strong one. Remember that if you are not properly insured the insurance company will pay only a percentage of the cost of a replacement stock.

Finally, there is the question of security. At the time of writing, the Home Secretary and various police authorities are proposing a rigorous tightening of the laws concerning the acquisition of a shotgun and the general opinion seems to be that it should be as difficult to obtain a shotgun as it is to apply successfully for a firearms certificate. The uproar and concern is a direct result of two separate incidents in which guns were used in public places with tragic results. The first occurred in August 1987, when Michael Ryan shot sixteen innocent people in the small market town of Hungerford; the second occurred in October of the same year when four individuals were killed with a shotgun in Bristol. The subject of the easy availability of shotguns is naturally of concern to those who are involved with any aspect of the media and, as a result, by the time this book is published I am certain that the authorities will have restricted shotgun ownership to shooters who can prove a genuine, legitimate need.

At the present time, however, security is simply a matter for the individual but, in an effort to show that the majority of the sporting fraternity is responsible in its handling and care of weapons, it behoves everyone to take the greatest possible care to make sure that guns are kept securely, not only at home but also when you are travelling.

The area in which I live is a rural one where shotguns are used by keepers, farmers and sportsmen alike, but the local police report an alarming number of cases where such people leave their guns in full view of the general public while their vehicles are parked on the highway and their owners call at the nearest shop for a newspaper or cigarettes.

With police-approved gun cabinets on sale through the sporting press costing as little as £49.95, there can be no excuse for such a lax attitude towards personal loss and other people's safety while you are either at home or travelling to and from a sporting estate.

5

Gamekeepers

Their changing attitudes ...

'Gamekeepers undoubtedly are often unpopular. In general they seem to have the reputation of being surly and morose, even of being downright rude and tough.' So wrote Brian Vesey-Fitzgerald in his book *British Game* (1946).

There are occasions, forty-two years on, when I suspect that the general public's opinion of a keeper remains the same. They continue to look upon the keeper in the same light as Vesey-Fitzgerald, who described the old-time gamekeeper as being 'uneducated, frequently brutal ... The only knowledge of natural history [which] he was expected to possess was the ability to distinguish a hooked beak ... and his work was usually judged by the number of corpses he could display upon his gibbet.'

Such opinions are wrong and are usually born of ignorance. Keepers and keepering methods have changed beyond recognition over the past twenty or thirty years and it is definitely a change for the better. The type of keeper described at the outset of this chapter has almost disappeared from our countryside and, hopefully, no employer will tolerate the kind of man who is still of the opinion that anything with a hooked beak is bound to be harmful to the pheasant stocks. Whereas eighty years ago the first requirement on the keeper's imaginary job specification would have been 'vermin control', it is now more than likely to read 'diplomat'.

The whole structure of estate life has changed greatly from the times when the gamekeeper was second only in importance to the landowner and spent his time riding around the shoot on a well-bred cob, his hands clothed in white kid-gloves. Having reached the dizzy heights of head-keeper, he would most probably have never worked again but instead would merely delegate to one of the many underkeepers in his direct employ.

Nowadays, however, there are estate agents and farm managers vying for such a delegatory role and the keeper and shoot are often relegated to the bottom of the list. Farming practices quite rightly take precedence, as it is from these that the owner receives most of his income and he is unlikely to do more than pay for his own sport on estates where the shooting is let.

The diplomatic keeper, therefore, must get on well with the farm and other estate-workers and he will do well to overlook the inevitable problems caused by farming operations and remain on good terms with the agent or farm manager, thereby ensuring that cover crops will be planted when and where they are required.

The keeper must also be able to mix with a variety of people now that many large estates have been split up and sold, the owner retaining only a small acreage over which to shoot. Much of the ground adjoining what were once estate houses and which have been sold off to private individuals, would be useless without good relations with the new owners. Co-operation with regard to blanking in or picking up can often benefit potentially poor boundary drives.

Just as the selling of ground has changed the pattern of the countryside, so too have modern farming operations. The loss of the hedges and woodland and the reduction in acreages owned by one man, has meant a reduction in the number of keepers as well as imposing financial restraints. Even in cases where the estate size has remained the same and the family fortune has been stable, the estate is unlikely to employ more than two or three keepers, whereas in the past there may have been half a dozen or more. Obviously, there are several other factors to consider. Modern labour-saving equipment and more intensive rearing, for example, have meant that one keeper can look after many more birds than would have been possible in the days of rearing with broody hens.

Number of keepers

Disregarding the growing army of part-time and amateur keepers, it is unlikely that there are more than seven thousand keepers in full employment today. It is interesting to compare this fact with the figures for fifty years ago, when it was estimated that ten thousand keepers were professionally employed. The numbers may not seem to represent a great decline, but in percentage terms it is more striking (a 30 per cent reduction), especially if you consider the overall population increase during those fifty years.

There are still keepers who, although they have changed their ideas in other matters, persist in hiding on the estate in the hope of deterring trespassers by cultivating a frightening image. Indeed, the head-keeper with whom I started my career advised me to shoot any of the villagers' cats and dogs on sight, stating that 'you'll get the blame for their disappearance anyway, so you might as well do it ...'

Excellent though this keeper was on other points, I think that he was wrong to harbour such an attitude and I have found that taking a dog back to its owner after catching it in a wire or informing them of its whereabouts on the estate, will earn more respect and co-operation among immediate neighbours than would a more aggressive and antagonistic attitude.

Likewise, a friendly 'Hello, you look as if you're lost . . .' if you see people walking miles from the footpath which inevitably runs through the estate, is likely to achieve better results than a tirade of four-letter words. There will, of course, be people who do not want the right of way pointed out to them and then may be the time to assert your authority.

To be a successful rearer of game, the keeper needs to have a certain amount of technical ability and to put a great deal of thought into an efficient rearing programme. In such cases, it is not impossible for a single-handed person to rear and release as many as 12,000 pheasants, 4,000 partridges and several hundred duck on to a 2,000-acre estate and give his employer 34 shooting days throughout the season by means of let days, syndicates and private days. This is not necessarily an admirable example, as large releasing programmes often give a 'chicken farm' effect on a shooting day, but it does show that such an operation can be carried out by one person.

... and their duties, month by month

Traditionally, the end of another shooting season sees the start of a keeper's year. What few offers of employment there are will have been advertised in the sporting press or by word of mouth. Some keepers may be successful in obtaining a position elsewhere but, for the majority, they will be content to prepare for yet another season on the same estate. With the ever-decreasing number of estates, most of which are reducing their staff, and the ever-increasing armies of do-it-yourself enthusiasts taking up what shooting is still available, there is much to be said for being employed by someone you know. It is doubtful whether the days of the early seventies, when it was possible to pick and choose any number of keepering positions from the numerous Situations Vacant columns of the shooting magazines, will ever return.

FEBRUARY

February is one of the best times of year for the keeper who will still be buoyant as a result of the success of his shooting season and will also be able to forgo some of the more mundane tasks such as regular feeding. Of course, if he still has birds to catch for the laying pen, then a regular food supply will have to be maintained along the rides until he is satisfied that he has enough birds to give him the required quantity of eggs, but there will no longer be the worries of wandering birds or the problem of finding sufficient drives as the season draws to a close to make a reasonable last shooting day.

Even with all the birds caught up, it will pay to continue feeding them in order to maintain a stock of birds which may hatch and rear a few 'free' poults during the course of the summer, but this need not be on a regular basis and a few hoppers, old straw bales topped up with the sweepings from the floor of the grain store or a hand feed every other day will be sufficient.

There is still plenty of time to attend to repairs on the rearing field equipment and to get the release pens ready, but the keeper should begin to make plans. A discussion with the boss while the past season is still fresh in everyone's minds may well result in some improvements being made. These could be nothing more than half a day spent in the woods with a chainsaw, but in some cases it will be necessary to employ a contractor to look at any problems and the decision to do so should be made when there is still plenty of time in which to implement any improvements.

Holidays

Most keepers take their holidays in February, especially if they do their own incubating, when a break in the milder weather would be impossible. A holiday is a good idea: a keeper who, through necessity, spends much of his year on the estate, unable to get away because of the demands made on him by his avian charges, will return in a better frame of mind and be even more determined to make the coming season the best one ever.

February also gives the keeper a chance to repay the regular beaters with a little close-season shooting. For many, the annual beaters' day or cock shoot will have been their only opportunity to get their own guns dirty. Now that the season has come to an end, they can shoot a few pigeons coming into roost or, in a hard winter, on the strips of kale which have been used as game cover.

MARCH

In March, Fenn traps should be dusted off and reset and

fox-wires placed in every available safe run, for now is the time for the major spring offensive against all forms of predators. Several legal traps made to catch stoats, weasels and rats are on the market, but the most commonly used is the Fenn Mk 4.

Hedgerows are excellent trapping sites of vermin as are the woodlands, but the choice of sites in the latter can be confusing. Tree roots, faggot piles, culverts, ditches and perimeter hedges all provide good positions but it is often necessary to make up an artificial tunnel where no natural material exists. Their construction is time-consuming and the keeper who sets off in the early morning, game-bag full to over-flowing with traps and wires, is unlikely to be able to put out more than a dozen of each before lunchtime. Many keepers feel that it is a mistake to continue setting traps and wires after lunch as they believe that the human scent will still be lingering when dusk approaches and the predators begin to move about.

Keepers who catch up hens and incubate their own eggs can find much to occupy the afternoon and early evening, which is the best time to set traps for catching up laying birds. The pheasants will be hungry after their day's wanderings and be more than eager to fill their crops before going up to roost. When the keeper is sure that it is too dark to catch any more birds and thus risk leaving them overnight to be killed by foxes, he will put the pheasants in sacks before taking them back to his vehicle and placing them in crates.

Weight and size of individual birds is very important and any small or undernourished hens will be returned to the wild. Cocks will be selected as large as possible.

Most keepers use a large communal laying pen in which to house their stocks. Because they have no overhead cover, it is necessary to deter escapees either by clipping the primary feathers on one wing or by brailing one wing. There are two types of brailing: with leather straps that are fastened by means of a paper fastener, or with ring brails (a circle of nylon tape) that is slipped over one wing with one or two flight feathers pulled through. This forms a figure of eight and keeps the wing in a closed position.

Egg numbers
Each hen will lay between thirty and forty eggs and a ratio of eight hens to one cock will provide fertile eggs later in the year.

Towards the end of the month, the keeper will begin to feed breeder's pellets rather than the last of the wheat to his laying birds. This balanced ration ensures that the hens will lay the maximum number of perfectly formed and fertile eggs.

At about this time, the incubator should be run up to the correct temperature and checked for faults. These machines are capable of holding anything from three thousand to about twenty thousand eggs and are fully automatic. Humidity and accurate turning are just as important as a constant temperature and it is well worth having the machine serviced by a professional.

Inside the incubator are rows of trays held in place with clips that are painted red, white and blue. Usually, incubators are filled on a Friday, one third of the total number of trays being set at a time. This job is done each week until the incubator is filled with the three different colours.

The eggs stay in the incubator for twenty-one days, then they are taken out and transferred to small hatchers for the last three days. While still in the large incubator, the eggs are kept at a constant 99.9°F (37.7°C) with a giant paddle forcing air around them. The hatchers, however, rely on convection to provide the air changes, with water providing the necessary humidity. By April, the first eggs should begin to appear in the laying pen.

APRIL

As the number of eggs increases daily, the keeper will need to stay close to home in order to pick them up as often as possible. Before long, the local population of rooks and crows will find that pheasant eggs provide an easily obtainable free meal. Such predators are capable of detecting eggs even when they are covered by the dense branches of fir boughs and straw bales placed as nesting cover within the pen. One way of dealing with the problem of predation is to use cage-traps, which also prove useful on other parts of the estate. Legal control of rooks and crows now falls entirely between shooting and cage-trapping.

The most generally useful type of cage-trap is a sectional one, approximately 6ft sq x 6ft (1.8m sq x 1.8m). By pre-baiting, the intended victims become thoroughly accustomed to feeding at the site before the trap is set in motion by closing in the roof and fitting funnels at ground level.

Predators

Predators continue to take up much of the keeper's time throughout this month. Foxes, stoats and weasels are running about, preparing for their own breeding seasons, and can be picked up easily in traps and snares. Picking up any enemies of game picked up at this time could prevent untold damage when the wild birds begin to lay or when the poults are first released into the woods.

The wise keeper will utilise any spare moments this month to prepare for the summer. By spring-cleaning and disinfecting the incubator shed, by checking the chick heating equipment and by using any available time to repair any winter damage that has occurred to the release pens in the woods, the keeper can avoid last-minute panic.

MAY

Unless the keeper intends to rear birds bought from a game farm at six weeks of age – in which case no rearing equipment is necessary – at the first opportunity he should consider preparing the rearing field ready for his day-old chicks.

Most rearing systems utilise calor gas as a source of heat, although existing outbuildings and an easily obtainable electricity supply can also provide the necessary heating.

For those birds fortunate enough to be reared by gas and on grass, the rearing field is usually set up in the following manner. First, a plywood shed measuring 8 x 6ft (2.4 x 1.8m) is erected, with a night shelter protruding from it. The shelter is made of four wire-netting sections with board around the bottoms; struts are then placed across the top of the sections, which are joined with electric fencing-wire to form a square, and then a sheet is tied over the roof space to provide a waterproof, windproof edifice.

After ten to fourteen days, the chicks are usually let out from the night shelters into larger open-air runs measuring 30 x 30 ft (9 x 9m), with nets placed over the top to prevent them from escaping.

Some keepers, because of lack of equipment, need to incubate in two separate stages and will therefore have chicks hatching off at the very beginning of this month. With the laying birds to tend, incubators to check, chicks to feed and water, the rearing field will have to be erected as and when time allows.

May is usually the best time to plant any game-cover crops which will be needed on the shooting days. In a normal year, the weather will be mild and the soil will be sufficiently warm to ensure successful germination.

The ploughing, preparation and planting of game-cover crops are usually carried out by the estate when the farm is 'in hand' but it may be necessary to employ contractors when the shoot is only rented or a tenant is in residence. It is not unknown for the keepering staff to be responsible for planting cover crops, but shoots where this is expected are few and far between.

The most commonly grown crop for pheasants is kale, but if the situation is warm enough to grow maize, or a mixture of maize and millet, there is the added advantage of providing a food as well as cover. Artichokes, mustard and canary grass all attract pheasants and will give some good drives early in the season before the frost renders them useless.

JUNE

With intensive rearing methods, most keepers will have to deal with feather-pecking during the six weeks that poults are on the rearing field. The condition is often a result of boredom or stress and certain young birds are singled out for attack by their companions, which leads to large losses if preventive measures are not taken.

The most effective step is to fit 'bits' on the chicks at the age of three weeks. Bits can be made of plastic or metal and are inserted between the upper and lower mandible and are held in place by the bird's nostrils. Although bitting effectively prevents feather-pecking, the process of insertion or removal can be so stressful that some birds die, but a precautionary course of high-level antibiotics (such as Terramycin) administered in the drinking water a few days before bitting or taking poults to wood may help overcome the problem.

Weather conditions in June can either help or hinder the keeper as well as being a deciding factor in the well-being or otherwise of any wild stocks of game. Traditionally, it has long been held that the second week in June (Ascot week) will see the hatching off of wild broods of partridges; if the weather is cold and wet at hatching, not only will the chicks die, but so too will the insect life which is so necessary a part of the young partridge's diet.

Pheasants are more adaptable and may well begin to lay again if a first brood has suffered. However, where silaging is carried out, they are unlikely to have much success, whether they nest in May, June or July. By the time the second cut of silage is ready, many birds will have chosen to nest in grass

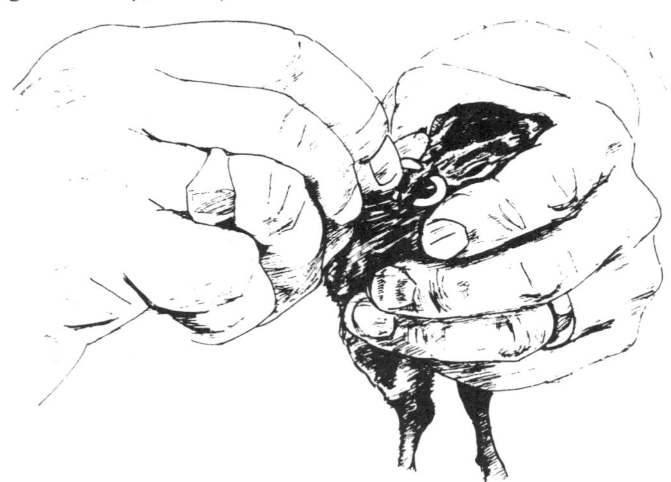

At the age of three weeks pheasant poults need bitting in order to prevent feather pecking.

crops and will be killed by mowers and forage harvesters.

Although this unnecessary slaughter of birds is well recognised, it is not easy to overcome. The keeper may feel that he is trying his best if he takes his dogs and flushes out the fields, especially the edges, before cutting of silage commences.

During much of the incubation stage, both pheasants and partridges emit greatly reduced scents as a natural defence mechanism against predators, so that even gun-dogs will have difficulty in locating sitting birds. Once the grasses begin to flower, pollen in the dogs' nostrils aggravates this difficulty.

On the rearing field, there could be problems other than feather-pecking when the weather is bad. Apart from the obvious misery to keeper, wandering knee-deep in mud and clad in Barbours instead of shirt and shorts, the cold, wet weather prevents any feeding other than in the sheds, is expensive on gas bottles and encourages disease. Coccidiosis is likely to be the most common complaint and wet conditions encourage its development. Fortunately, the disease is easily treated if caught in time and the astute keeper will expect trouble and be prepared for it.

JULY

If the release pens are not ready by July, the keeper is likely to encounter a few problems. Given plenty of time, the construction of a release pen is relatively simple: all that is required is some good, strong posts with small mesh around the base of the pen, preferably turned out to prevent any animals digging their way in, and topped off by larger mesh that is turned out to prevent the same animals from climbing in. A strand of electric fence-wire running all around the perimeter gives extra security.

As well as constructing a new release pen or maintaining and repairing an existing one, the keeper will need to spend some time on ground-clearance work in and around the pen. Some ground cover is essential, but it should be made easy for poults to find their way to the feeding area in the early stages: a newly released bird needs time to acclimatise to its surroundings and it can get separated from its companions and become lost in the release pen if the cover is too thick. Some bigger gaps should also be created and a few large trees can be taken out to remove some of the canopy and create 'sunning' areas, which the poults will certainly appreciate; they will take full advantage of such sunning areas after a shower of rain or as the day begins to warm up after a chilly night.

A release pen is a necessity because most of the carefully reared poults would die without one. An alternative name for the release pen could be 'acclimatisation pen' because this is exactly what it is.

When the birds reach the age of six or seven weeks (usually towards the end of July) the keeper will catch them up on the rearing field, remove the anti-peck bits, clip the ten primary feathers of one wing, put the poults into carrying crates and take them to the release pen. Ideally, the pen will contain enough varied growth and vegetation to keep the pheasants amused until the primary feathers regrow and they can fly out over the wire. This process should take about a month and the keeper will use this time to accustom his charges to a regular feeding routine. As the keeper takes the feed twice daily, he will whistle or make some other noise to tell the birds that their meal is ready. Very soon, no matter where the birds are in the surrounding woodland, they will return to the pen as soon as they hear this noise and can be walked back into its safety through specially designed anti-fox grilles and be secure until morning when, once again, they will fly out and explore a little more of their new environment.

Clearing up

As soon as the last birds leave the rearing field, the rearing equipment should be dismantled and stored in a weather-proof building for the winter.

AUGUST

Carrying water and food to the release pens will be a regular daily chore for the next few months. Where time allows, a little vermin control should be continued in and around the releasing areas.

Duck shooting

1 September also sees the start of the duck-shooting season. If there is water on the estate, the keeper will probably begin to throw down a little barley this month in order to attract a few wild mallard or teal on to the ponds and give his employer and his friends some extra shooting. If so, it may be necessary to make a few hides. Although it need only be the roughest of structures – a camouflage net strung over a couple of hazel sticks, for example – it is yet another chore to be fitted in around the keeper's main job of managing the pheasants.

The keeper who is responsible for a few partridges will need to utilise some of his rearing sections as makeshift release pens in and around the game covers, from which he hopes that they will fly to best advantage on the shooting day. It is usual to release partridges, whether they be French or English, at about a month before the first shooting day.

Because partridge pens are smaller (four 10 x 5ft [3 x 1.5m] sections tied together), it is possible to cover them with roof nets so that there is no need to clip the wing feathers. With the partridge season opening on 1 September, the normal procedure is for the keeper to put twenty-five birds into the pen and hold them there for about a fortnight. Then, as and when he feels ready, he allows one or two partridges their freedom until, after ten days or so, there are only a couple left in the pen. It is thought advisable to let this pair remain in the pen throughout most of the shooting season as they will act as decoys to ensure that the remainder return to roost each evening.

By now some of the earliest pheasants will be flying out from the release pen and will have to be persuaded to return if they are straying too far from home. The best way to do this is with dogs.

The breed and obedience of a dog are of secondary importance. In fact, a well-trained gun-dog is not recommended for the job because there is a risk that it may develop bad habits in the process. When pheasants wander in search of food they travel on foot, but they will take to the wing on the way back. The keeper takes full advantage of this habit and may even forgo the morning feed because he feels that regular dogging-in is more important. If poults are fed after they have been pushed back to the woods, they will be more inclined to stay where it is desired.

Some gamekeepers, however, feel that dogging-in can do more harm than good and argue that if a dog gets behind a group of, say, forty poults, ten of them will fly over the boundary, ten each to right and left, and ten towards home, whereas if they were left alone there is always the possibility that they will all return by late afternoon.

SEPTEMBER

Few keepers deal exclusively with partridges, but where several hundred have been released in order to have specific partridge days (rather than a couple of pens which are only expected to cause a pleasant diversion on a pheasant day) the shooting season starts early.

Beaters, guns and dogs are bound to have an adverse effect on the pheasant poults when it is necessary to drive a stubble fields situation between the releasing woods. Wounded partridges which fall in the woodland perimeter must be picked up and one cannot tell a dog, no matter how well it may be trained, to fetch the partridge and leave the poults alone. This all makes further problems for the keeper, who may already have troubles with disease in the release pen, or wandering pheasants, or foxes picking up birds as they fly out from the pen, or headaches caused by farm staff who, by now, are well engaged in harvesting operations.

If the evenings are dry, combining may continue until the dew falls. Because of this, poults may be prevented from returning home or are being disturbed as they attempt to go to roost. Apart from dogging birds back out of the way of machines, the keeper can do very little, but he may feel the need to stay and watch in order to make sure no harm comes to his precious charges.

Towards the end of the month, straw should be available from the farm for the keeper to being preparing his out-tracks. Birds cannot be expected to remain *ad infinitum* in the releasing woods, and indeed no one hopes that they will, because the release pens are often situated in places not likely to produce high, testing birds, but to provide a reservoir in surrounding game covers and woodland from where pheasants will fly well. Straw that has been spread along carefully prepared rides in these areas will help to encourage birds to treat both crops and woods as a second sanctuary from where they will eventually be pushed homewards over the guns.

For a start, the keeper will spread his straw and lay a minimal supply of wheat over the top. If there is too much, it will begin to grow before the poults find it but if correctly managed, with a little spread once a week at first and then every other day, it will not be long before pheasants are waiting on the feed rides. Every feed is accompanied by the familiar noise or whistle which the birds recognise from their time in the release pen and which helps to attract any indecisive pheasants that have been hanging around the edges so that they come in towards the feed rides where, hopefully, the keeper will have some control over them.

OCTOBER

If the keeper has succeeded in keeping his birds at home until October, they will probably remain for the rest of the season. However, if the autumn proves to be a bountiful one as far as woodland fruit and nuts are concerned, he will be worried when the pheasants fail to return for the evening feed. Although I have been keepering on a single-handed basis for nearly fifteen years, the autumn still proves to be a great worry and, after a poor feed, I can often be seen driving around the estate desperately looking for returning birds. I do not know where they disappear, but any Gun who asks the keeper how the pheasants are will be in for a pessimistic reply.

Some keepers have a dozen of so pheasants of differing breeds such as the Melanistic, Chinese or Buff variety, which they can use as marker birds. They can indicate where the pheasants are straying and they may be a comfort. In one particular case, a white cock remained in the pen long after most of the other birds had found their wings, until he decided to venture across the road, over which he soon went to roost (a sure advertisement to poachers). During the next three days, although I kept a careful look-out for him, there was no sign until I went to give the ducks on the flight pond their weekly feed and it was there that I noticed him on some barley tailing left over from the previous feed. Although only a short distance from the pen and my twice daily feed whistle, the bird refused to return home and was still in the same place the following week. The incident shows that, although the keeper may be experiencing poor feeds, all is not necessarily lost and the poults which he may have thought had wandered off could, in fact, be close at hand.

Some keepers who have worked on an estate for many years notice that birds disappear in mid-October only to reappear by mid-November when natural food starts to become in short supply. After a number of shooting days, some pheasants (usually cocks) will vanish from a wood at around Christmas time only to turn up at the season's end, resplendent in their breeding colours and pecking at the spring-sown corn, to the farm manager's annoyance.

The keeper will still be spending time refilling food-bins and topping up the water as well as trimming out tracks that will be needed later for sewelling and gun-stands. Gun-sticks need to be cut so that numbers can be wedged in the top to show the Guns where they should stand for each drive.

Sewelling is an important feature of the shooting day; without it, birds will run straight through the drive and provide a very poor target as they fly at the last minute rather than being made to take to the wing upon reaching the flushing point. With a pile of plastic fertiliser bags and a roll of baler twine, this can be avoided. Sewelling is made first by rolling up the bags and cutting them into 2in (51mm) wide segments, then by knotting them to the string and rolling it on to a drum from which it can be unravelled on shooting day and strung across the wood or game crop to encourage those birds running forward to fly to the best advantage.

Although the pheasant-shooting season officially begins on 1 October, it is unlikely that many shoots will begin any serious attempts before the leaves begin to fall in the early part of November.

NOVEMBER

As the first day of the season approaches, most keepers will find themselves either driving or walking around the estate with their employer, discussing the coming season. Some employers like to involve themselves with the positioning of the gun pegs; others leave it entirely up to the keeper.

It is preferable if the employer has a hand in the positioning of the gun pegs because if the shoot-owner or captain stands by a peg which he has previously used, he will probably be reminded of the time when the beaters came too far forward and pushed most of the pheasants back over the left-hand guns. In a large wood, there is no way that the keeper or person in charge of the line can tell what is happening far away from him, but the owner standing on his peg may see things of which the keeper is unaware and, when reminded of them on a pre-shoot preamble, he can plan to push forward an extra stop or arrange for one of the Guns' wives or girlfriends to be shown the spot and be asked to stand and tap.

Beaters, pickers-up, game-cart drivers and other necessary helpers need to be contacted and the keeper needs to spend several evenings on the telephone checking whether their services will once again be available. To all keepers, good beaters are important and it is essential to maintain a regular and reliable team.

DECEMBER

In the eyes of most keepers, December is very much a 'non-month'. It seems that the shooting season has only just got under way when, as Christmas approaches, it is almost over with only another month to go. The daylight hours are so short that there is very little time left after feeding to do more than prepare for another shooting day or help neighbouring keepers on their days to ensure that the favour will be returned. Probably the only real advantage is the fact that it is no longer necessary to carry water for the birds as the pheasants have long since left the pen and can have a drink wherever and whenever they like.

After a few shooting events, the birds will be wary of

returning to where they were disturbed but, provided that the keeper continues his feeding routine, they will eventually answer to the whistle again.

Poachers

Although pheasant prices from the butcher leave much to be desired, it is a lucky keeper who is never bothered by poachers, especially as Christmas approaches and the demand for birds increases. Unfortunately, feeding the birds and a few necessary chores must be carried out before the keeper can relax for a few hours over Christmas lunch.

Many estates maintain the tradition of a Boxing Day shoot and, even though it is mainly a 'fun day' for the Guns' families and a chance for them to walk off the results of their over-indulgence, the keeper still needs to prepare the day as carefully as he did for some of the big shoots in late November.

JANUARY

The keeper who hatches his own eggs will by now be thinking about catching up. Even though there may be a few more shoots to take place, if there is a particular feed with a large proportion of hens, the keeper could well begin catching up in order to prevent too many birds being shot. Where possible, this is a wise precaution because, although there may be only one or two official days left, it is an unusual estate which does not add at least one extra shoot before handing over to the keeper, beaters and farmers so that they can fit in a day's sport before the season finally comes to an end.

These 'cock' or 'keepers' days are intended to thank all the helpers for their assistance during the season. Although there will be very few birds left in January, every effort should be made to ensure that the keepers have as good a day as possible and it will be much appreciated if the host and the regular Guns are prepared to turn out and beat for them. At the very least, a special lunch or a few bottles of whisky which can be passed around at the end of the day should be provided by the shoot.

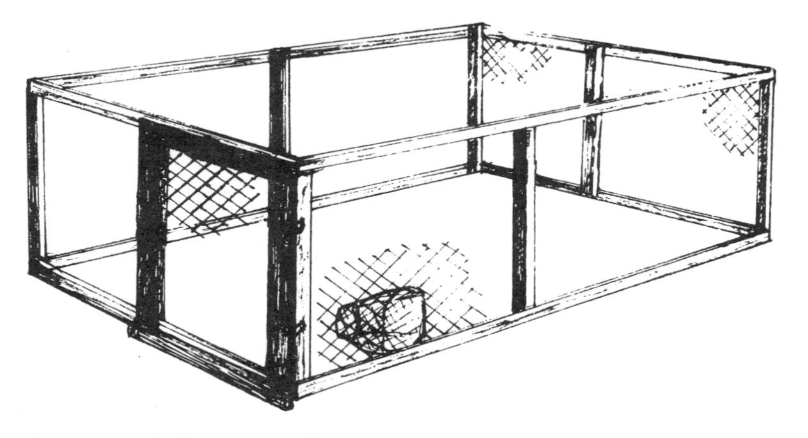

One type of pheasant catcher. Note the 'funnel' which allows the bird's entry when looking for food, but prevents exit once caught.

Even before the season has ended, the enthusiastic employer will call his keeper into the office to discuss the season and bag totals, and possibly to suggest a few improvements which he would like the keeper to carry out during the ensuing months. Thus the keeper will begin another season and, before he knows it, he will be preparing once again for the arrival of the young chicks.

The grouse keeper

Many employers feel that every keeper is a grouse keeper – if there is any problem they will grouse about it! But the type of keeper I am talking about are the ones to be found in the North of England or Scotland and may be encountered by the Gun who is tempted to try some of this country's most exciting shooting on the moors.

The grouse-moor keeper's duties bear no resemblance to his lowland counterpart. In the first instance, it is not possible to rear grouse artificially and then successfully release them into the wild. The grouse keeper's main job, therefore, must be to ensure that the wild stocks have every possible chance of survival.

The grouse moor

To be worthy of the name 'grouse moor', the area needs to be at least 2,000 acres, containing plenty of good heather and very few vermin.

Any keeper is, or should be, keen to rid himself of predators which are likely to damage his game-bird stocks when they are at their most vulnerable. Today's keepers, no matter what their responsibilities, tend to control vermin as and when required rather than when they see, for example, a fox killing it. They therefore put themselves in the position of being accused of 'blanket killing'. The fact remains, however, that it is probably more important for the grouse-moor keeper to be in control of his vermin problems than it is on the low ground where, if the worst happens, someone somewhere will be able to supply pheasants or partridges to replace any losses.

Foxes, crows and stoats pose the greatest problems to the grouse keeper. Unlike his counterpart on the low ground, who has woodland to help him approach his quarry unseen, the moorland keeper has few such aids and often has to rely on drainage schemes or long heather in order to get close enough with a gun. Traps, however, catch predators even when the keeper is asleep and prove to be a vital asset in controlling stoats. One would think that small animals would fare badly in moorland country but, against all the odds, they seem to thrive.

Being curious creatures, stoats are easy to catch and a few Fenn or box traps set into the base of any stone wall will help enormously in their control.

During my time on the grouse moors, the head-keeper considered trapping to be the most important part of my duties and he stressed the need to look out for potential fox earths while I was on my rounds. Snaring for foxes is virtually impossible on the moors as there are no well-defined runs and the only hope of coming to terms with a moorland fox is by waiting up with a gun near to where it is expected that a fox will emerge. In the winter, when snow is on the ground, it is often possible to determine which hole a fox is using by following his tracks homewards and this is one reason why the grouse keeper's kennels are likely to contain a veritable collection of terriers and only the odd gun-dog. The terriers will be working for most of the year, and will be gun-dogs for only three months.

Foxes have their favourite earths and most moorland keepers know of a hole where they can enter their terriers and be almost guaranteed a shot as the fox bolts.

Just as important as predator control is the correct management of the heather. Since grouse use heather for cover as well as for food, the keeper must provide both long and short heathers in a patchwork effect throughout the entire moor. This is best achieved by burning on a rotation basis but, by law, this must only be carried out at certain times of the year. Generally, heather burning is restricted by the Hill Farming Act of 1946 to the period 1 October–15 April and, although this covers a seven-month spell, the actual number of days when the operation can be carried out is limited because of damp weather or because the keeper is engaged in other duties. The best rota for burning is on a twelve to fifteen-year cycle and correct burning will provide good feeding for both grouse and sheep.

It is an acknowledged fact that a moor which is good for grouse is also good for sheep and if there were no grouse, management would not generally be up to the same standard. There is, of course, much more than putting a match to the heather and hoping for the best, and the efficient keeper will burn his ground on a rotation principle in the same way that an arable farmer plans which crop is going to be grown in which field.

Very often as a result of an unhealthy interest taken in butts by sheep, who use them as a shelter from the worst of the weather, the keeper needs to spend much time in repairing and building the estate's butts. The stands in which the Guns are placed while grouse are driven over them can vary considerably in shape and size, from a short straight wall behind which a Gun can stand, to an elaborate design which affords plenty of room in which to accommodate the Gun, loader, guest and dogs.

Where possible, grouse butts must be situated in a straight line for extra safety. Where one butt cannot be seen from another, a peg is best driven halfway in the line. The peg will undoubtedly be used as a rubbing post by sheep and so must be checked immediately before a shooting day.

The traditional start to grouse shooting is 12 August and, because of the importance of the date in the social calendar, most estates make a start as near as possible to that date.

Not only will the keeper have checked that the butts, access roads and so on are in pristine condition, but he will also have visited the local farming, forestry and shepherding communities enlisting their help as beaters. Because of the scarcity of human population in grouse-shooting areas, this task is not always as simple as it might be to the low-ground keeper.

The ever-increasing spread of bracken may mean that there is a great deal of back-breaking scythe work to be carried out in the immediate vicinity of the butts if there is to be any hope of guns and pickers-up finding what has been shot. Ideally, bracken cutting should be done as early as possible before the shooting season commences as newly cut bracken gives off a smell which nullifies the scent of fallen game.

A regular supply of grit for the birds is often neglected. Although there may be a seemingly abundant supply already on the moor, it is not necessarily the right kind. Quartz or granite grit is best and the keeper will find that its regular provision helps keep his birds at home.

Finally, you should remember that the idyllic setting which has been described for August, with the keeper in his shirt sleeves, silhouetted by acres and acres of purple heather, lasts for only a short time. Within a few months, the landscape could well be covered in several feet of snow with a wind literally strong enough to blow you over. It needs a dedicated and enthusiastic man to continue working in these conditions, but the moorland keeper must do so if there is to be any hope of a successful shooting season next time around.

6
The Gun's Dog

It is unlikely that the tyro or casual Gun will require his own dog for the occasional foray into the shooting field, but there is no doubt that, as his interest grows, he will consider the acquisition of a canine companion.

Traditionally, the game-shooter's dog was a retriever of birds only. The dog was trained or, rather, 'broken' by the estate's head gamekeeper, to sit close to the stand and not to move until the drive was over, when it was then expected to pick up dead and wounded birds from around the peg.

At the beginning of this century, labrador retrievers were almost unheard of and the dog of the day was either a flat-coat or curly-coated retriever. It was also more common to see pointers and setters rather than spaniels on the shooting field and they were used extensively on the partridge manors, especially in areas of small fields and large hedges where a covey was likely to disappear out of sight as soon as it was flushed. Horace G. Hutchinson described the methods used in Devon when he edited *Shooting* in 1903:

> But the covey is a rare and precious thing; by all means, it if be possible, to be rediscovered and shot again. Therefore it was sometimes the plan to have a man on horseback accompanying the shooting party, whose mission was to sit like an equestrian statue on top of the nearest hill, and thence to mark down any covey that was flushed ... shooting them over dogs is the best alternative. Dogs are useful in finding you birds when they are scarce, and so saving your two legs by their four legs.

The situation in the shooting field has changed tremendously since then and, possibly because of the surge of interest in re-introducing breeds which have been taken over by the show world and in importing continental types of gun-dog, there are probably more trained gun-dogs working in Britain now than ever before.

The newcomer to shooting is bound to notice the preponderance of labradors and spaniels and will obviously be able to recognise them. He may, however, be puzzled when it comes to identifying some other breeds which are beginning to appear, so it could be useful to describe briefly a few of the most popular minor breeds as well as looking at what is required of both spaniel and retriever.

The Labrador

Unlike its early twentieth-century counterpart, the modern retriever is expected to do much more for its owner than sit quietly at the peg until the shooting has finished. The popularity of the labrador undoubtedly stems from the fact that it is trained both quickly and easily (hence the great demand for them as guide dogs for the blind and as 'sniffer' dogs to discover illegal drugs). Unfortunately, the breed is divided into three sections or, to be more precise, the owners form the points of a triangle. Some wish to work their dogs in the field; others are content to stimulate their animals' instincts by means of working tests, while the remainder wish to exhibit in an effort to win cups and rosettes.

Watch out!

One pitfall is that the would-be purchaser of a dog which he hopes eventually to work in the field replies to an advertisement or responds to word-of-mouth recommendations (given in good faith) only to find that, at a later date, the breeding is incorrect. The labrador is probably the only breed where this is likely to occur; in all the others, show and working stock are easily differentiated.

To have any chance of catching a trout, one must first of all take time to master the basics of casting. Unfortunately, all too many newcomers to shooting expect to be able to buy a gun and take it onto the field without any form of tuition (Graham Simpson)

The accepted and safe way to carry a gun when it is not actually in use...

...unfortunately, it is not uncommon to see a gun carried in this manner and, if one happened to be standing on the next peg, it would undoubtedly give cause for concern (Gina Arnold)

Shooting is not just a matter of killing as many birds as possible and, for those interested in dog work, it gives them the opportunity to put early training to the test (Barrie White)

The Lake Vyrnwy Hotel: one of the many sporting hotels which offer a wide variety of shooting (By courtesy of the proprietors)

Wildfowlers are more concerned with keeping warm and dry whilst waiting for hours on end in wet ditches, than they are in sartorial elegance. For them, good waterproofs are essential (Gina Arnold)

Guns and alcohol do not mix and even the beaters need to exercise some restraint when the hip flasks are being passed round prior to driving home (Barrie White)

It is often better for the Guns to travel in one conveyance rather than use their own four-wheel vehicles, as too many individual motors could present problems (Barrie White)

Good pickers-up are essential if no birds are to be left wounded at the end of the day (Barrie White)

Although the flanker may sometimes appear to be taking life easy, his knowledge of just when to show himself and wave his flag at a covey of on-coming grouse, can often make the difference between a successful drive and an unproductive one (Gina Arnold)

A person specifically in charge of bringing birds in from each drive will more than pay for himself as well as easing the pressures on the keeper when it comes to sorting out the least damaged pheasants to give away as gifts at the end of the day (Barrie White)

Today's keepers no longer look upon anything with a hooked beak as being detrimental to their pheasant stocks, and the only thing likely to appear on their gibbets (if such things still exist) are winged vermin such as crows and magpies, or stoats, weasels and squirrels; the latter of which not only take eggs and young chicks but also damage forestry plantations and cause problems to the farmer's cereal crops (Gina Arnold)

The laying pen should contain plenty of cover in which the hen birds can lay their eggs without attracting the attentions of crows or other egg-eating predators (Gina Arnold)

The rearing field complete with brooder houses, night shelters and outside runs (Gina Arnold)

Day-old chicks need to be contained close to the warmth by means of corrugated or hardboard surrounds which ensure that they do not stray too far away from the heat source. Easy access to food and water is also essential (Gina Arnold)

It has long been known that certain farming operations can prove detrimental to any wild bird stocks. Silage making for example, is bound to destroy both hen birds and eggs which are often situated in grass crops at this time of year (Gina Arnold)

Clipping the first ten feathers on one wing of a six-week old poult will prevent it leaving the release pen before it has become used to its surroundings and the keeper's whistle (Gina Arnold)

Poults must be allowed to walk out from the carrying crates in their own time and will immediately begin to explore the new surroundings (Gina Arnold)

The flat-coated retriever is one of the minor breeds currently enjoying a revival amongst the shooting fraternity....

...as too are some of the continental all-rounders: in this case a German short-haired pointer retrieving a dummy at full speed (Graham Simpson)

Part of the grouse keeper's duties includes the maintenance of the butts which vary greatly in design from moor to moor. The half-rounded, turf-topped stone-built edifice seems to be the most common (Brian Hobson)

'Most of today's resident population of Canadas result from escapees from private collections.' They are now, however, quite common and it is not unusual to locate a nest of eggs on a shoot which contains even the smallest amount of water (Gina Arnold)

Sometimes an adult tawny owl will be panicked into flying forward through the activities of the beaters. Identification of an individual species is often made more difficult when late-hatched birds show themselves in immature plumage (Gina Arnold)

'Fortunately, the shooting world is full of characters and friendly faces' (Barrie White)

A group of eight-week-old French partridges in the holding pens. The hand-rearing of partridges has led to an increase in the amount of birds seen both on the shooting field and in the bag at the end of the day (Graham Simpson)

At the end of the day it is far better to have an area set aside specifically for the dog rather than it be squeezed in among shooting gear for the journey home (Author)

A sunny corner is the ideal location for the positioning of gundog kennels (Author)

It is unlikely that the pickers-up will be in position and ready for the next drive when the previous one has shown a lot of birds. When they do eventually surface, however, they will not be empty-handed (Richard Hedger)

The end of a successful September day (Geoff Burch)

With the labrador breed being divided into three different groups, it is imperative that the buyer ensures that a particular breeder has maintained the dog's inherent natural working and game-finding ability. He should also take into account temperament and ability to be trained. Assuming that all these points have been considered and that adequate training is given, the average labrador should be capable of being a very efficient working animal.

There may be some shooting purists who are still content to see their dogs sit without being tethered while they themselves pick and choose the highest flying pheasants and drop them with apparent ease within yards of the peg. When the keeper blows his whistle to signal the end of the drive, a flick of the fingers is sufficient to ensure that the labrador will leave his mark and rush around stylishly retrieving anything within sight. Most keepers try to ensure that gun rides are trimmed out at the beginning of the season and so these shot birds will, in all probability, have fallen in full view. Why, then, is it necessary to have a dog to do what a little leg work and back-bending can achieve?

Pricked and wounded game rarely falls within 20yd (18m) radius of the pegs and a dog which picks up only in this circle is useless. Shot birds tend to fall 200yd (182m) rather than 20yd (18m) away and many will remain unaccounted for if the dog cannot be directed to this sort of distance. The Gun who shoots only driven birds must realise this fact and make sure that his retriever is capable of finding them at this distance.

Apart from its success rate as a retriever, the labrador is chosen by almost every type of shooting sportsman because of its versatility. There is considerable interchange between the roles of labradors and spaniels – which is surprising if you consider that one is a retriever and the other a flusher of game – but labradors of the right breeding are equally at home pushing out game as they are at bringing it back once it is shot. The rough shooter is more likely to choose them in preference to spaniels because they are easier to train and, as a rule, training must be fitted in around work and home life.

Gamekeepers like to include beaters in the line who are

also owners of labradors because they know that the dog is more likely to be capable of being stopped when a flush occurs. They also know that, after a particularly heavy drive, when there are too many shot birds for the picking-up team to cope with, they can transfer the beater and his dog to help out with picking up before calling them back into the line when the next drive is too thick to manage without the aid of the dog.

The pigeon shooter will probably choose a labrador in preference to any other breed because it can be relied upon to sit quietly in the hide, without constantly moving around which would cause any overhead bird to veer away well out of shot. Nor will the labrador crash blindly through the nearest gap in the hide when it is sent to retrieve. The wildfowler favours the breed for the same reason and in addition labradors are excellent swimmers. They can swim better than any other variety of gun-dog; they react quicker to changing currents and have extra power from their 'otter's ' tail. Their coat seems impervious to the wet and cold and, unlike a spaniel or other long-coated dog, is not susceptible to becoming covered with icicles on a cold January morning. The wildfowler's dog must often withstand hours of icy wind both before the first shot is fired and after a successful retrieve.

No matter what the labrador's position, it must be capable of marking any fallen birds. After all, it is first and foremost a finder and retriever of game. To create a good marker, experience is essential as well as good training. I once had a dog which I used extensively for picking up: it would sit quietly by my side for most of the drive but then, without warning, it would run in. Invariably, it would return with a pricked bird which, to the Gun who had shot it and myself who had been watching closely, often looked as if it had flown through the line unscathed. That sort of marking is perhaps impossible to teach and can only be learnt from experience, but it seems that such gifts are becoming fading skills, with increasing numbers of dogs relying on the handler to point them in the right direction.

Springer spaniels

The two types of springer spaniel – English and Welsh – are essentially the rough shooter's dog. They are capable of hunting through the thickest cover all day and yet still have the energy required to find a dead bird when game has been shot.

Which type?

Of the two types of springer, the English is the one most commonly seen and used. Both are similar in height and build, so the easiest way in which to differentiate between the two is by means of colour. English springers are predominantly white with liver or black markings, while the Welsh is only ever white with chestnut (commonly known as 'red') colouring.

The Welsh have been condemned by spaniel enthusiasts for many years on the grounds that they are more likely to yap when putting game out of cover, whine when they are waiting for a drive to terminate and are more prone to being hard-mouthed when they retrieve. Yet there seems to be no one actively involved in the gun-dog world who is actually prepared to state that these generalised opinions are facts and it is thought by the Welsh springer spaniel enthusiasts that those who hold such opinions are only quoting those which they have read in books and the writers of those books are only passing off what they have read in other publications.

Understandably, this hearsay is very annoying for owners of Welsh springers. It is a fact, however, that the breed is harder to train and can often seem somewhat wilful and pig-headed. Once trained, the springer has the advantage of a better nose: when an English and a Welsh are working together, it is noticeable that the English will work through the thickest of cover even when there is nothing there, while the Welsh will enter only if there is something to be flushed. The Welsh springer is not, perhaps, as stylish as the English, but that should not worry any owner unless he intends to enter his dog in working tests and field trials. The fact that

The working springer is generally of lighter build than those bred for exhibition or showing. They are not usually very tall on the leg and have less feathering which would very soon become clogged with mud or debris from the undergrowth. Most breeders also prefer to leave a longer tail when docking litters of working parents, feeling that they are more stylish to watch and show up in cover. To leave them undocked could result in the tail being continually split open when pushing through cover...

Welsh springers are generally steadier should more than compensate.

Nevertheless, English springers continue to dominate the shooting field. Beaters who are sufficiently interested in dog work tend to choose an English springer to work in the beating line because they know that the dog can also prove an invaluable aid when they do a little pigeon shooting out of season or attempt to catch up with pheasants released on their own patch of rough shooting.

Professional gamekeepers tend to favour the English springer spaniel because of its thrust and adaptability. No other breed of dog can be expected to accompany the keeper quietly around his trapping line in March and April, plod around the rearing field when the young chicks arrive and yet ignore them once they begin to fly out of the release pen. When the birds travel too far, the keeper's spaniel is often called upon to dog them homewards and, once the shooting season begins, must be capable of hunting in the line as well as picking up on the neighbour's shoot. In February there may be some rabbit control to be carried

. . . probably the most obvious difference between working and show breeds are the unusually long ears found on the show type

out and a steady spaniel will need to flush rabbits from thick cover but still treat ferrets emerging from a bolt-hole with great care.

One problem which the rough shooter is likely to encounter is the increasing non-availability of suitable cover in which to train his dog. The Gun who shoots only driven game and yet chooses a spaniel as his companion compounds the problem and very often lacks the interest or knowledge to handle his dog correctly, with the result that many modern springers seldom experience this essential part of spaniel behaviour. There is no other way in which the handler can stimulate his animal's full potential and to use a springer merely for picking up is a waste of its inherent talents. By the time the dog has achieved the peak of its retrieving capabilities, having been trained to pick up birds which it did not flush, it has ceased to function as a spaniel. The owner, therefore, might have bought a retriever instead.

On the other hand, it may just be a fact that such an owner prefers spaniels to any other breed, even though he intends to use the dog for a purpose other than that for which it was bred. In such a case, it would be foolish for an owner to buy a retriever when he knows, in his heart of hearts, that he really wants a spaniel. He will never be satisfied with anything other than a spaniel and the dog he buys will never fulfil his expectations.

Cockers, clumbers and field spaniels

The real spaniel enthusiast has several alternatives when it comes to choosing a breed which is ideally suited to his needs. All spaniels require different approaches on the part of the handler and it is a fact that the three breeds mentioned in this section need very careful handling.

The cocker is a pretty and attractive dog and it has been the subject of much heated discussion among the members of the gun-dog world. From being a very popular and useful adjutant to the shooting day, the cocker spaniel suffered a considerable decline in the early 1960s when it fell out of favour with most professional gun-dog trainers. Peter Moxon, probably the most articulate and thought-provoking trainer and writer of the last twenty years, was quick to notice the failings of the working cockers and was not afraid to write of what he saw. It says much for the man when, in recent articles, he has been prepared to admit that the breed is progressing well and he gives successful contestants in field trials glowing reports.

His adversary on many occasions is fellow trainer and writer, Keith Erlandson, whose prefix appears in the pedigrees of most competent working cockers and features in the final three of the largest field trials, thus proving both his obvious knowledge and the fact that, when a breed has problems, there is usually someone who can be relied upon to fight for its well-being.

Keen handlers, therefore, make the choice of a minor breed that much easier and it is interesting to note that, when helping out on neighbouring shoots, cockers are taking their rightful place among the echelons of springers already in the beating line. The owners do, however, have to tolerate questions (mostly from the Guns) such as how old is the puppy. On being told by the handler that he animal is three years old and fully trained, the questioner usually disbelieves the answer.

Many reasons have been put forward to explain the cocker's revival. Its decline was probably linked to the nationwide demise of rabbits when myxomatosis took effect, but if the springer could adapt to pheasants, why not the cocker?

Some experienced handlers hold that specialised breeding by a few minority owners has ensured the cocker's popularity as a trial dog. The dog's success gives the would-be owner a chance to see the breed at work and it is only my personal interest in the English springer that has prevented me from owning a cocker.

Most experienced handlers, no matter how dedicated to the breed, agree that the cocker is not an ideal first dog as it needs very careful training and vigilance during the first couple of shooting seasons if it is not to develop incurable bad habits. A young springer at this stage can be re-shaped by taking it back to its basic training, thus correcting any faults.

On the grouse moor

Correctly trained, the cocker can prove to be the ideal companion for those Guns intending to shoot on the grouse moor where, on a hot day, it has an undoubted advantage over, say, a springer. Because the cocker's skin area is greater in proportion to its bodyweight, the heat loss is greater, so, in theory at least, it should be able to continue working for that much longer in warm weather.

When asking a keen judge of working tests for his opinion on the clumber spaniel, I was told that they have no style, but, to the rough shooter, this might be an advantage and the breed's undoubtedly slower pace but unsurpassable nose would make it an indispensable companion on a shoot where game is scarce and therefore hard to find.

Unlike most other breeds of spaniel, the clumber is apparently very slow to mature, both mentally and physically, which is perhaps not surprising as the standard weight for the breed is 80lb (36kg) for a dog and 65lb (29kg) for a bitch. In an effort to be taken seriously, breeders are now preparing for the future by attempting to develop a lighter, smaller and therefore more active dog which is more likely to want to please its owner rather than itself. Perhaps by doing so they are laying themselves open to the allegation that the breed will be far removed from the type which was to be seen in the last days of the nineteenth century, when it was not unknown for packs of clumbers to be taken out as beaters, but it must be better to see a breed continue, even if in name only, rather than to disappear into obscurity.

Much of the above applies equally to the field spaniel and to the Sussex spaniel. The latter breeds also suffer from the same derogatory remarks made by owners of the more conventional breeds. I have heard such owners say that the Sussex is prone to give tongue when on a scent. In fact, this was once thought to be a desirable asset because it gave the owner the opportunity of following his animal through the thickest of cover. Continental shooters still favour a dog which will give tongue when on a scent and I am told that there are more Sussex spaniels to be seen in Europe than there are in this country, for that very reason.

Identification

The clumber is easily identified as it is basically creamy white; the Sussex is only ever a golden-liver colour, but the field can be self-coloured black and liver, roan or tan, or even mahogany red.

Golden, flat-coat and curly-coated retrievers

Of the three minor but increasingly popular types of retriever, the golden must be the one most often seen on the shooting field and is as easily recognisable as the labrador. Like the labrador, the golden possesses both game-finding ability and trainability. Although it is claimed by many devotees that the golden retriever can be encouraged to hunt and flush game with the tenacity of a spaniel as well as acquitting itself by retrieving on the most formal of shoots, such a paragon is, in my opinion, a rarity and the ones which I have seen working lack style and dash when covering the ground.

Admittedly, golden retrievers have excellent noses and will

eventually find a pheasant crouching in the thickest of cover, but when they are being handled in the beating line, it is not usually possible for the keeper to hold up the line in order to give the dog the opportunity to quarter at its own pace.

The golden does, however, have one great advantage over labradors when it is used as a retriever by the Guns or pickers-up. I have already pointed out how difficult it can be, for those who use their labradors only to fetch shot birds from around the peg, to get them out sufficiently to retrieve pricked game several hundred yards away. Goldens, on the other hand, seem to take in more ground naturally when casting around for a shot bird and so demand the minimum of attention from a socialising or otherwise preoccupied Gun.

Goldens also have the advantage, because of their higher head carriage, to pick up an air scent on difficult scenting days rather than having to rely merely on the scent that remains on the ground which is the method other breeds use.

The golden is renowned for its soft mouth, which should make it a popular choice for the person who intends to use the dog solely for picking up. The golden must be encouraged to return quickly once it has picked up the bird for which it was sent, otherwise there is a risk that the dog can develop sloppy retrieving habits.

The working flat-coat is a different proposition. The tyro needs to take particular care if he decides to purchase a flat-coat puppy as there is very little difference between the show and working sections. Fortunately, it is rare to find even a show-bred animal without a slight trace of working ancestry. The flat-coat should hunt and retrieve as well as any other type, but at working tests and field trials (the only time I have seen the breed at work) they fail to show any real promise. This situation may soon change now that the Working Flat-coated Retriever Group has been formed. With one of its aims being to provide a register of breeders who can guarantee that their stock is of true proven blood, future breeding may ensure that a considerably greater number of flat-coats will be seen on the shooting field and will compare favourably with some of the usual breeds.

Identification

Confusion often arises in differentiating between the curly-coated and the Irish water spaniel. Both are comparable in height, weight and shape, but a certain way of telling them apart is by means of colour: water spaniels are liver while the curly-coat is only ever black.

I mentioned at the outset of this chapter that the curly-coat was the favoured dog among both Guns and keepers at the turn of the century. Indeed, when I was employed as a keeper's boy at the start of my career, the head-keeper with whom I was fortunate enough to work felt that the curly-coat was the only true gun-dog. In his mind, the curly-coat was a one-man dog which was devoted to its handler and very rarely returned from a retrieve without bringing back its objective. He remembered that not only was it an excellent gun-dog, its determination ensuring that it would succeed at any task, but it also proved an ideal companion as a night dog in search of poachers.

As with many other minor breeds, it is up to enthusiasts to ensure that the curly-coat returns to its former glory but, with labradors and goldens fulfilling all that the Gun is likely to ask of them the chance of their revival is uncertain.

Continental all-rounders

There are numerous breeds which fall into the category of continental all-rounders. They are expected to hunt, point and retrieve, but it seems that only a few prove to be real assets on the shooting field, and then probably only to the rough shooter.

The fact that the all-rounder is required by official standards to 'hunt for game, point and hold it long enough for the Guns to position themselves ...' immediately limits their use in the beating line when it is hoped that the drive contains many birds. In theory, with pheasants tucked up in every available area of cover, any member of the hunting, pointing and retrieving fraternity (HPRs) would still be on point at the beginning of the beat when the keeper blows his whistle to signify the end of the drive. In practice, however, it seems that this is not the case and I have seen German short-haired pointers working on both pheasant shoots and on the grouse moors and, what is more, making an excellent job of it.

Upon scenting a bird, the German short-haired pointer does, in fact, point and hold its point but as it is not required to hold it for long – there being no Gun to prepare himself – the handlers encourage the dogs to flush almost immediately. It might be expected that, after a certain period, the dog would realise that the flushing of the bird was the most important aspect of its job and begin to omit the pointing side, but (and I have discussed this question with every handler I have met) it appears not to be the case and even ten-year-old animals with a lifetime of formal beating behind them still hold a point long enough for their owners to be aware that game is in the immediate vicinity.

The German short-haired pointer is probably the best known of the various breeds, but I do not know whether it is because they are the oldest continental type in this country (they were introduced shortly after World War II) or because they have proved to be the best workers of the various breeds on offer.

Unlike its cousin, the German wire-haired pointer, which, as its name suggests, possesses a 'broken' coat (thought by many to be an advantage in heavy cover or wildfowling conditions), the short-haired has a very fine, silky coat. Both types can be liver and white, black and white or an all-over liver colour.

Until recently, the Hungarian Vizla and the Weimaraner were the only alternatives for the Gun who wished particularly to own an HPR but, although they have both been available for about thirty years, they have for one reason or another failed to catch the shooting person's imagination. The Vizla is short-haired with colouring of varying shades from honey-blond to russet-gold, while the Weimaraner is silvery-grey (for which an early outcross to the great Dane is said to be responsible).

A recent and serious contender in the fight for 'top

continental dog' is the large Munsterlander, which was the subject of much discussion in the popular sporting press when it first appeared in Britain in the early 1970s. Visitors to any of the many county shows or mini game-fairs may have seen individual representatives of this breed and mistaken them for black-and-white English springers with undocked tails. The Munsterlander is, in fact, closely related to the long-haired German pointer and, with its coarse coat and strong swimming action, could prove to be the ideal wildfowler's dog.

Buying a dog

Having decided which breed to choose, the Gun must then select his own dog. Whether his eventual choice is one of a puppy or a more mature animal depends to some extent on his family and business circumstances.

It is a reasonable assumption that if a person can afford to pay for a season's shooting as a member of a syndicate on an individual estate, or can avail himself of the numerous opportunities offered by sporting hotels and agencies, he can afford the £400–£500 necessary to buy a mature, fully trained gun-dog. After all, it is no more than he would pay for a well-made shooting suit which will last for only three or four years, while, with careful handling, his dog should be capable of serving him well for eight to ten years.

A fully trained dog is the only reasonable choice for a man who expects to be away from home for a considerable amount of time and will not have the chance to take a puppy out for its daily training sessions. If bought from a professional trainer, the dog will almost certainly have spent its entire life in an outdoor kennel and will expect and look forward to its twice-daily exercise. Obviously, there needs to be a family member willing and able to take charge of exercising the animal when the owner is away from home, but apart from regular exercise and a daily feed, the kennel-bred dog requires very little attention. This does not mean that it can be neglected, but it certainly causes less upheaval to family life than would a puppy living at home.

A fully trained dog should only be bought from a reputable

trainer and preference should be given to those establishments whose kennel prefix appears as a common denominator in the pedigrees of known friends' animals. In this way, you can see how an individual performs and, with luck, you can expect your own dog to behave in a similar fashion. Even though field trials are not necessarily indicative of a good shooting companion, trainers who indulge in such competitions do at least show that they are on the right lines, especially when they feature frequently in awards.

The age at which a mature dog is offered for sale depends entirely on the animal's character: some are receptive to training from the age of around six months whereas others are still too puppyish at this stage and need to be left until they are capable of taking in what is being taught. Generally, however, a fully trained dog would be about eighteen months to two years old before appearing in the 'Dogs for Sale' columns of the sporting press.

Take care

Advertisements which state that a dog is 'partly trained' should be treated with caution: a dog needs only to obey the command to sit to be described as partly trained. Other dogs that have been trained in a reputable establishment may have fully grasped the basics and only require finishing off with some real work on the shooting field.

The description 'an ideal rough-shooter's dog' – usually applied to a three or four-year-old spaniel – should be treated not only with caution but with suspicion as it usually (although not always, and I apologise immediately to those who sell genuine well-trained, rough-shooting gun-dogs) indicates that an animal has not quite made the grade. This is more often the fault of the handler than the dog itself but, nevertheless, if you do decide to purchase such a dog in a moment of weakness, it is inevitable that problems such as running in to shot or fall will occur. These misdemeanours may not seem so great on paper but perhaps you should imagine yourself standing beside the peg with a newly acquired dog by your side only to see it break free in an effort to retrieve a bird, become waylaid by a fresh scent of an unwounded pheasant which happened to pass the same way during blanking-in operations and take itself off to the nearest cover in an effort to recapture the scent. Inevitably, it will discover some unshot birds and take itself off on a wild abandoned chase, destroying carefully planned drives for later in the day.

Take good advice

As in the case of buying a second-hand car, the potential dog owner should take with him someone who is experienced in gun-dog handling who knows what he is looking for when the animal is being put through its paces by the vendor.

Choosing a puppy

Choosing a puppy from a litter at seven or eight weeks of age is not easy. At this stage it is virtually impossible to pick out an animal which is guaranteed to make a good, biddable shooting companion and the only real guide is to pick an animal which catches your eye.

There are many ideas put forward as how to make the best choice. Some people advocate throwing a rolled-up handkerchief and seeing which puppy is the first to try to retrieve it; others say that you should rattle a box of matches or clap your hands to see which animal shows the most interest. Another way may be simply to notice which puppy is first out of the box and comes to meet you, while yet another person may suggest taking all the puppies out of their box and buying the one which the bitch tries to carry back to the nest first.

It is not necessary to describe the individual characteristics of each breed because the dog will be perfectly formed and will be immediately recognisable as true to type as soon as you see one that catches your eye.

Gun-dog breeds should possess a dark eye and the majority of trainers will advise you to avoid an animal with a light or yellowish 'hard' eye.

Like the purchaser of a mature dog, the Gun viewing a litter of puppies should ask to see the parents' pedigrees which will, hopefully, contain a few field-trial champions or winners. However, if any have appeared in the show-ring it is best if they go back to the great-grandparents' generation, because although it is possible to find a show-bred animal which has made a good worker, there is no point in buying a dog from pure show stock when plenty of working lines are available.

Some of the retriever breeds, notably the labrador, suffer from hip dysplasia (HD) or retinal eye problems (PRA) and many reputable breeders therefore offer veterinary certificates which state that their dogs have been tested and found to be free from either disease. Advertisements in the 'Dogs for Sale' columns sometimes state, for example, 'All dogs Cert PRA, x-rayed HD,' or, 'All have PRA/HC (eyes clear) certificate', which helps the individual to make his final choice.

Dog or bitch?

Whether you intend to buy a fully grown dog or a puppy, there is the added question of which sex to consider.

If there is already a family dog in the household, then the decision to buy a puppy of the same sex is generally the right one. With a dog and a bitch in the same house, there is bound to be trouble when the bitch comes in season. Even when kept carefully apart, a bitch is frequently successful in finding her way to a mate during the vital mid-oestrum period, while a dog can also prove a determined escapologist when the smell of a bitch on heat is in the air.

The neutering of dogs and bitches helps to overcome these problems, but spayed bitches and castrated dogs tend to put on excess weight because their hormone balance has been upset. There are also those who believe that either operation causes a change of temperament, making an animal sluggish and less alert, but there is no sound veterinary proof to confirm this.

In my relatively short keepering career, only two bitches have passed through my kennels – one a labrador, the other a terrier – and I was not successful with either animal. The terrier is now a household pet that only occasionally forays after rats, while the labrador was sold because I could not get her to work with any real enthusiasm even though I spent much time with her and had her in the house from a puppy. A couple of months later, I saw her working with her new female handler and had to look twice because she seemed a totally different dog.

No theory can be based on such a short acquaintance with two bitches but, in comparison, I have had four male animals and have had to pass on only one. I feel that, for me at least, dogs work better for men, bitches for women – contradicting what many, much more experienced handlers than myself believe, that 'opposites attract'.

Perhaps the would-be buyer should assess his own character before deciding whether to opt for dog or bitch because the most important factor must be the temperament of the handler. Some people require a dog in preference to a bitch because they are themselves a little impatient, quick-tempered or heavy-handed, and the male of any breed can usually cope best with such training. There are always exceptions to every rule and it is possible to find a dog with a 'bitch nature' (indeed, the spaniel I am working at the moment is a prime example) and vice versa.

Dogs or bitches with too gentle a nature are often accused of being less forceful in cover than would be an animal with a more aggressive temperament. I feel strongly enough about this to dismiss the idea as being completely foolish: any gun-dog worthy of the name will thrash its way through the thickest of cover or retrieve a bird from the coldest of water, even though it may also be happy nuzzling into the lap of its owner in front of the fire on its return home.

It is an interesting fact that bitches are definitely more popular than dogs. This may sometimes be because, at the back of the buyers' minds, there is the possibility that they can recoup some of their initial financial outlay by breeding at a later date. However, whatever the reason for the preference for bitches, breeders now charge much more for bitches than for dogs – a complete reversal of the old days when breeders would put down some bitch puppies because they knew that they would not sell.

In the end, however, the choice is a matter for personal preference and experience.

Professional trainers

The Gun who is successful in business may not have the time to train his own dog and, in an effort to own a perfect animal, could decide to send his puppy away for some professional training.

If he can afford it, it may pay any first-time gun-dog owner to seek professional advice, even if it is only by enrolling in training classes organised by the local gun-dog club. It is a common saying in the shooting world that 'before you have a good dog, you have first of all to ruin one' and perhaps advice from those who know a little more could help prevent even your first dog from being spoilt.

Many trainers specialise in only one or two breeds, so it is best to ensure that the kennels which you may be considering do take in the breed of your choice. It is possible (though not, I hasten to add, in a reputable establishment) that business may be slow and the trainer will agree to take on a dog of a type which he knows nothing about purely for financial reasons.

Dogs will often do better in a professional kennel environment than they will if trained at home with all the inevitable distractions. Dogs feel secure with a regular routine and this is what they are offered in training establishments. All handlers have their own way of doing things, but most exercise and clean out first, take the dogs out for a short training period and then exercise again later in the day. Feeding times vary from place to place, but the practice of feeding at lunchtime, with a quick run around the grass paddocks immediately following, seems to me to be a good one, allowing the dog to empty itself and thus encouraging kennel cleanliness.

With such routines, the dogs know exactly what is happening and look forward to the regularity of exercise and training sessions. From the handler's point of view, he can watch them at all times and, when out with the dogs, will not allow himself to become distracted, which is very important when he is trying to establish himself as the 'pack leader'.

The handler must be constantly in command as he needs to gain the animal's respect so that it will follow instructions, watching and listening to all the handler's movements and words until it learns that it must work in a certain way that does not displease the 'leader'.

When the trainer feels that he can do no more with the dog, the Gun should go in person to pick up the dog from the kennels and take the time to go through all the verbal commands, hand signals and whistle variations which the trainer has impressed upon the dog. Not all training sessions are successful, however and occasionally handlers, no matter how good they are, have to reject an animal which they feel will never make the grade, rather than allow the owner to waste any more of his money in fruitless future training.

All too often, those who do not fully understand canine psychology make the mistake of thinking that, because their dog has been trained by a professional, it will maintain its newly acquired high standards right through its shooting career. Unfortunately, nothing could be further from the truth and the owner needs to be aware of the necessity for constant vigilance. He could start by keeping his dog on a lead before and after each drive, when it is all too easy for concentration to lapse or a distraction to occur as even the best of animals will misbehave when they realise that you are not paying attention to them. Do not, however, build up your own concentration to a point where it becomes stressful because the dog will quickly sense your tension.

A final and very important point to remember when re-establishing a relationship with the dog when it returns from the trainer is that an instant response to commands and instructions should be encouraged. If the dog does not respond quickly, he is less likely to listen to any amount of shouting of 'Hup!', 'Sit!' or whatever, and it is better not to give an instruction if you cannot enforce an instant response. Once he has been checked, get him into a stationary position and start again, lavishly praising him when the command has been carried out correctly.

Take care
Remember that a dog is either trained or it is not and there is no in-between stage, despite what other owners whose dogs may not be up to mark might tell you. I have seen dogs in my beating line and dogs belonging to my employer's friends which ruin a drive because they are not given sufficient time and attention.

After-shoot care

At the end of the day, whether the dog has performed well or not, it deserves careful attention before being returned to its kennel, especially when it has been involved in wildfowling or picking up game on a particularly wet and windy day. The working life of a good gun-dog is short enough without abbreviating it through neglect. At the end of a cold, wet day, make sure that you dry the dog as quickly as possible because a dog that dries off slowly can develop rheumatism and other ailments.

Before leaving the shoot at the end of the day, it is important to dry the dog roughly. This can be done in several ways. You can use either an old towel or a chamois leather for the job. When I did a great deal of loading for a previous employer and travelled from shoot to shoot in his Jaguar, I would carry a hessian sack in which I put my spaniel, leaving his head protruding from the opening at the top. This had several advantages: first, it kept the interior of the car clean, secondly the dog's body heat was retained which helped to dry it off and, thirdly, his sitting and lying movements over a long journey resulted in friction between sack and hair which successfully removed mud and other debris. I see from advertisements in the sporting press that it is now possible to buy purpose-made bags which are tailored to fit individual breeds, the price rising with the size of dog. Perhaps I should begin marketing old corn sacks as being the 'ultimate dog drier – fits all sizes'.

If a towel or leather is used to dry your dog and the animal is then allowed freedom of movement in the back of the car, you could place newspapers on the floor to absorb any further moisture and dirt. (Newspapers are very useful to the dog owner: they can be used as prescribed above, or as bedding for an in-whelp bitch, or they can be torn into strips to serve as a warm and comfortable substitute for straw in a kennel's sleeping-quarters. In the latter case, newspaper also has the advantage of being less vulnerable to the attentions of minute parasites which will irritate the skin and annoy the dog.)

Most people have a few offcuts from rubber-backed carpets in the attic and a piece of this cut to shape and placed on the floor of the vehicle is almost as good as a layer of newspaper. It has the advantage of being not quite as slippery, it lasts longer and can be removed and cleaned with a stiff brush.

For those owners proud of their cars, there are fibreglass fitments which help to contain mud and dirt. However, without adequate floor covering this in itself will not help with the drying off process and the units are also expensive to buy. Anyone with a modicum of carpentry knowledge could build a much cheaper alternative from plywood and wire mesh and, unlike the bought product, it will also keep its occupants confined and warm on the journey to and from the shoot. It also prevents the dog from eating the gift brace of pheasants which the keeper often places in the back of a vehicle while its owner is still in the house enjoying the host's hospitality.

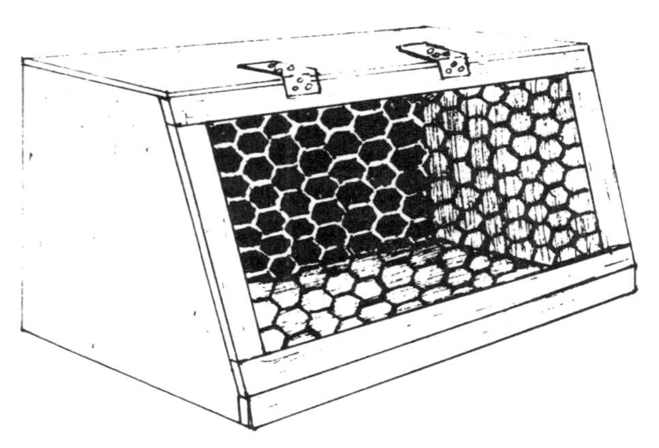

An easily and cheaply constructed 'dog box' which, when fitted into the rear of an estate car, will help in keeping the interior free from mud and hair

If the shoot owner has organised lunch, it is a good idea to carry food and water for the dog which will probably be returned to the car while the guests adjourn to the dining-room. Water is more important than food as too much of the latter may leave the dog lethargic and unwilling to work during the afternoon drives, while to feed it immediately prior to the return journey could result in even a well-travelled dog becoming sick. Too much water taken at one go when the animal is exhausted can have the same effect, so take care to ensure that the dog goes not drink too liberally.

If the dog is not completely dry upon its return home, further rubbing with a towel may be necessary. If there are several dogs, it could pay to follow the example set by some hunting packs and put aside a small shed full of dry straw in which the dogs can spend some time rolling and drying off before they are returned to their kennels.

A word of warning

Never be tempted to allow a wet dog free access to an open fire as it will draw out the coat's natural protective oils. Unusually excessive heat is detrimental to a kennel dog when it is returned to its cold quarters at night.

The Gun who takes a day's shooting as a guest of a sporting hotel could well have minor difficulties with regard to drying his canine companion. It seems that most sporting hotels have no objection to dogs sharing the guests' bedrooms, but few have real kennel accommodation. Drying off a dog in these circumstances often requires some initiative, but a towel and newspapers can help provided that its sleeping quarters are dry – an easy matter when you are sharing a bedroom but not quite so simple when the dog is expected to spend the night in the car. The dog which is used to being kennelled is probably better off than one which spends its life within the home environment because the animal's natural skin secretions will ensure that the oils in the guard hairs will repel any moisture before it reaches the more delicate down next to the skin.

7
Game Laws and Bird Identification

There are some thirty-nine bird species at which the Gun can shoot but in this chapter I will give only a general layman's guide to some of the many complex laws which concern the taking of game.

There is, for instance, the often quoted example of a person who accidentally runs over a pheasant. It is an offence for that person to pick up the dead pheasant, but it is permissible for the next person on the scene to acquire the carcase. If a dead bird which has been shot by legitimate guns falls into the road and is picked up by a casual passer-by, it can be said to have been stolen while 'in the course of being reduced into possession' – ie the Gun himself or a picker-up would otherwise have collected the carcase.

Most keepers know that, once their carefully released pheasants have left their woodland pen, they no longer belong to anyone and therefore cannot be stolen (they are then subject to different laws and can be poached) but, conversely, at the end of the season when the birds are caught and prevented from escaping, they become private property and are thus capable of being stolen.

The game laws are complex and even though the majority of them were written in the eighteenth century (with the exception of those amended in the Wildlife & Countryside Act of 1981) many still apply.

Generally, the right to take game is the prerogative of the owner of the land on which they stray. The owner may, of course, give authority to other people to take game, provided that they abide by the government's rules and regulations regarding close seasons and game licences.

If the ground is let to a tenant, the sporting rights automatically pass to him unless, by written agreement, the owner reserves the rights for himself: when working out such an agreement it is advisable to use specific terms – ie 'shooting' or 'sporting', because to restrict yourself to 'game' only can often leave you without the right to 'wildfowl', for example.

The sportsman's quarry

The regular game shooter restricts himself to nine game-bird species: pheasant, grey or French partridge, red or black grouse, ptarmigan, capercaillie, woodcock and snipe.

Duck are often included among the sportsman's potential quarry but they are, in fact, wildfowl, of which, once again, nine species are permissible: mallard, teal, pintail, shoveller, gadwall, tufted, pochard, wigeon and golden-eye. Four species of goose may also be shot: pink-foot, greylag, white-front (not Scotland) and, probably the most common, Canada.

All wildfowl may be shot inland in the period 1 September to 31 January, but the shooting season on estuaries is extended until 20 February. As we shall see later in this chapter, identifying these species in the half-light, when they are most likely to be on the move, takes some competence, but wing and vocal sounds, flight patterns and silhouettes will all help you to recognise them.

EEC directives

In 1986, shooting (and indeed field sports in general) was brought to the attention of the European Parliament following the formation of a group with the rather long-winded title of 'European Parliament Intergroup for Field Sports and the Environment'. The organisation consists of members of the European Parliament from nine countries and six political parties, all of whom are prepared to defend legitimate field sports.

Although any favourable attention is to be welcomed, unfortunately Europe seems to be somewhat hesitant to offer grants which would help the British shooting community in its conservation and management work. At least one further point is left open to misinterpretation, namely that, despite the fact that our own Wildlife and Countryside Act defines a shotgun with two rounds in the magazine as meaning two cartridges in the magazine and one in the chamber, the EEC Commission interprets the statement as meaning two cartridges in the gun. It is very confusing and the whole issue could perhaps be dismissed as being yet more European Parliament waffle, were it not for the fact that the general consensus of opinion among members of the European Parliament Intergroup for Field Sports and the Environment is that *legitimate* shooting is of benefit to the countryside in Europe and is 'an integral part of conservation'. For example, the 1979 Birds Directive has been the guideline by which the European Court of Justice is now charging certain countries for failure to ensure that *only* 'legitimate shooting' is carried out. From this one assumes that the mass slaughter of songbirds being shot on their migration through Europe by machismo-obsessed Mediterranean *cacciatores* is still being carried out despite its being outlawed, so any group of people, whether they are based in Brussels or elsewhere, must be applauded for taking a strong stand.

Keepers generally appear to be against the EEC because of minor difficulties caused by yet another of its directives. It is no longer possible to pick up the telephone and order rearing food without first going through the time-consuming procedure of obtaining a prescription from the vet to include certain necessary preventative drugs in the food's manufacture.

Game licences

A tax on the killing of game was first introduced in 1784. The act, which was made law in 1831 and amended in 1860, enforces those of us today who wish to shoot game to take out one of the four types of licence which cater for the various open seasons for game birds. The different times of year call for colour-coded licences, costing £6, which are available from the Post Office.

Without a licence, it is an offence to

> ...kill, take or pursue, or assist in doing so, by any means whatsoever, or to use any dog, gun, net or other engine for the purpose of taking, killing or pursuing any game, woodcock, snipe, rabbit or deer without the appropriate licence.

There are certain exceptions to the above rule and these include shoot helpers such as beaters, loaders and pickers-up who are assisting a licence holder. Gamekeepers, too, are exempt provided that they are in possession of a keeper's licence and are shooting on their employer's land. If they are invited to an end-of-season cock shoot elsewhere, then it must be assumed that they need to take a trip down to the Post Office in order to obtain the more usual type of licence.

Having bought your colour-coded piece of paper, it pays to keep it in the jacket of your shooting attire as you must be able to produce it immediately when asked to do so by a member of the police force.

In Northern Ireland, the open season for pheasants permits the shooting of cock birds only, unless evidence of releasing hens can be produced, in which case a further licence to shoot hens must be obtained from the Department of the Environment at Stormont Castle. Incidentally, all species of geese are totally protected in the Irish Republic, as are moorhens and coots.

Take note

Even when you are in possession of a valid game licence, you must not attempt to shoot at any game species on Sundays or Christmas Day.

Although hares are covered by the Ground Game Act, and so a shooting tenant would not require a game licence, they too must not be killed on Sundays or Christmas Day, even though in Great Britain there is no close season for the taking of hares on arable land. For those who wish to shoot moorland and similar unenclosed areas, hares may only be shot by the occupier and persons authorised by him between 11 December (1 July in Scotland) and 31 March. It is also illegal to sell hares or offer them for sale during the period 31 March–1 July inclusive.

Some open seasons

Although most people know that grouse shooting begins on the Glorious Twelfth (of August) and that pheasant shooting opens on 1 October, it may be of academic interest to include a brief list to which the reader can refer. Famous though the 12th is, how many know that the season ends on 10 December or that one is allowed to shoot pheasants on 1 February and that the season does not close the preceding evening?

Grey and red-legged partridge: may be shot in the period from 1 September to 1 February.
Ptarmigan (Scotland only): 12 August to 10 December.
Black grouse: 20 August to 10 December.
Capercaillie (Scotland only): 1 October to 31 January.
Woodcock (England and Wales): 1 October to 31 January (Scotland): 1 September to 31 January.
Common snipe (Jack snipe protected): 12 August to 31 January.
Golden plover: 1 September to 31 January.

The Wildlife & Countryside Act (1981) permits authorised persons to shoot the following 'pest species' at any time except on Sundays and Christmas Day on which days the Secretary of State has expressly forbidden shooting:

Collared dove	Jay	Herring gull
Wood pigeon	Jackdaw	Great black-backed gull
Feral pigeon	Carrion/Hooded crow	Lesser black-backed gull
Magpie	Starling	
Rook	House sparrow	

Hard-weather bans on wildfowl

Even though a ban on the shooting of duck in hard weather may seem unnecessary when one rears and feeds duck on the estate and can thus keep them in tip-top condition, nevertheless waterfowl which are dependent on finding their own food source can suffer greatly in times of severe weather.

Birds such as woodcock and snipe can feed only by probing soft earth or mud and they will lose weight dramatically if a few days of unbroken frost prevents them from doing so. Their natural instinct helps them find unfrozen feeding grounds, notably in the milder western parts of Britain and Ireland where, in a normal year, the least amount of frost is likely to occur.

If woodcock, snipe, duck and geese find suitable feeding areas and are then harassed by shooting operations and the inevitable disturbances, their chances of surviving a particularly severe spell of hard weather are greatly reduced. The true sportsman would refuse to go out and shoot any bird which is obviously declining in physical condition, but the sight of dozens, if not hundreds, of wildfowl congregating around a patch of unfrozen water, less cautious than usual, could prove too much of a temptation to the more unscrupulous shooter. Consequently, in a prolonged spell of bad weather, the law must intervene.

Before the government ministers stipulate an obligatory shooting ban, they are involved in discussions with the Nature Conservancy Council, the BASC and other shooting and conservation organisations. Because the latter can be expected to have a better understanding than could a government department, they are in an excellent position to advise when and how a ban should be effected. Selected weather stations throughout the country, which monitor the exact degree of freezing temperatures, are also contacted and the information is used in reaching a decision.

Unfortunately, ensuring that the government's decision reaches the ears of the shooting public is no easy matter. Although the bans are published in magazines such as *Shooting Times* and are mentioned occasionally on the radio, very often the first that you hear of a legal disruption of your sport is via a friend. The ban could have been in force for several days by then and might have been you breaking the law by innocent indulgence in an evening flight. Far better, then, to observe the weather carefully and impose a voluntary restriction on yourself if things look bad.

From past experience, it seems that a ban imposed by the government generally lasts from a week to a fortnight, after which the situation is reviewed and, if necessary, the ban renewed.

Gun safety and the law

Anyone with a modicum of common sense would never intentionally shoot towards a road, footpath or house but, apart from the fact that it is an offence to shoot within 50ft (14.1m) from the centre of a public highway (a law that was made so that horses, which were the only form of transport at the time, would not be frightened), there are surprisingly few laws which deal specifically with such incidents.

If, in the heat of the moment, a person did shoot towards a property, accidentally shattering the roof of the householder's greenhouse in the process, and the police were subsequently called, then a prosecution would have to be made under the Criminal Damage Act to bring that person to court. Even then, for a prosecution to be successful it would have to be proved that the defendant had failed in 'taking responsibility for his actions'.

Basically, then, you should always think first and fire

second. It is easy enough to write such advice but it is not quite so simple to follow it when you are following through the line and your mind shuts out all but the target and the required lead. Nevertheless, if a severe accident occurred that involved injury or even loss of life, you can be certain that, no matter what the circumstances, the media and the general public would assume that it was the Gun's fault and the incident would succeed in banging yet another nail into the coffin of sporting shooting. In all probability, if the accident took place at a driven-bird shoot, the participants would be labelled as 'Hooray Henrys' with more money than sense. It would matter little if, in fact, the person in question was on the minimum weekly wage and had saved all year to be able to buy one day's sport from an agency. Even a pigeon shooter on someone else's land by permission would find that the press had elevated him to the position of landowner in an effort to make their headlines more sensational.

If shooting is to continue, it is in everyone's interest to abide by the rules even when there are very few directly appertaining to gun safety and the law. It may, therefore, be a worthwhile exercise not only to read the 'dos and don'ts' which are printed on your shotgun certificate but also to imagine the possible outcome if you were responsible for an accident – minor or major, it matters not, as once you are out in the field warning bells should ring in your brain and prevent imagination from becoming reality.

Bird identification

Identifying the larger game bird species is not difficult. Although the flight of the woodcock can be either strong and swift or slow and weak, its twisting pattern and the fact that its bill is nearly always carried pointing downwards mean that it cannot be mistaken for anything other than what it is. Fellow Guns and beaters are not likely to let the advent of a woodcock go unnoticed and it will be rare for you to see the bird without first having heard their excited cries.

When the adrenalin is in full flood and a flush of birds is expected, it is all too easy to catch sight of sudden movement

Because of the similarities in flight, sparrow hawks are often mistaken for wood pigeon. Both frequent wooded areas and glide on their approach to cover; to shoot pigeon is legal but to shoot a sparrow hawk is most definitely not. By studying natural characteristics, the individual Gun should be able to avoid any mistakes.

in the corner of your eye and turn and raise your gun, only to find that the object is nothing more shootable than a blackbird or hedge sparrow. Fortunately, it is also easy enough to pull away from the target and refrain from shooting.

Distinguishing between a wood pigeon and a sparrow hawk is not perhaps quite so simple. While picking up, I have noticed on several occasions a Gun take a bird from his dog, look around and then throw it into the middle of thickest bush. Being of an inquisitive nature, I have then waited until things were quiet and put one of my spaniels into the same bush only to see it retrieve a sparrow hawk. The explanation is obvious: it is illegal to shoot a bird of prey, so the bird shot in error had been quietly hidden and forgotten.

The Gun cannot be faulted: the flight of both pigeon and sparrow hawk are indeed very similar. Because the latter is in the habit of suddenly swooping up and over a hedgerow or gliding with intermittent spasms of three or four wing flaps and then soaring before entering the wood with folded wings, it is easily confused with the former which, according to *Collins Pocket Guide to British Birds*, 'flaps upwards at a steep angle and then glides down with wings scarcely upraised'.

As everyone knows, owls rarely appear in daylight but, when beaters tap through the woods and bang their sticks at the base of an ivy-covered tree where tawny owls often spend the day, the birds often have no alternative but to fly forward over the gun line. Their slow, flapping flight should be sufficient to prevent the shooter from accidentally raising his gun, but it is all too easy to make a mistake because tawny owls are common throughout almost the whole of Great Britain (with the exception of Ireland and the Isle of Man). You should remember, therefore, the possibility of an owl coming forward in daylight and also bear in mind that further identification is likely to be aided by the noisy mobbing of small birds.

The *Collins Pocket Guide to British Birds* and Brian Martin's *Sporting Birds of the British Isles* make essential reading in the close season and they will undoubtedly help with identification in the field.

Wildfowling problems

One of the most difficult problems with identification concerns the singling out of wildfowl when you are out on an estuary or marsh. Because the majority of wildfowl arrive in the half-light, it is often possible to identify individual species only by means of their cries, particular movement and gregarious tendencies. The nine species of duck are totally different in habitat and behaviour from one another, but mallard – the most common form of wildfowl that are seen from the Chichester harbour to the estuaries of the Solway – need no special mention. Identifying others, however, could cause some problems, but perhaps memorising the following points may help you to identify each species correctly.

TEAL

Although the teal is similar in flight to the mallard, the movement is much quicker and the individual is more likely to respond to the actions of others in the flock by 'jinking' and performing fast collective manoeuvres, reminiscent of some of the wading species.

Because teal consort regularly with other surface-feeding ducks, especially mallard, it is probably the second most common species to be seen around inland waterways and its cry will often make identification that much simpler; indeed, *Collins Pocket Guide to British Birds* describes the sound of groups as a series of 'tinkling bell-like notes'.

WIGEON

The sound of wigeon is often all that the wildfowler has as a means of identification and causes evocative memories in the hearts and minds of old and experienced wildfowlers. They will tell you that the whistling of the drakes can be heard through the densest fogs and that the duck calls with a cat-like 'purring' tone.

Wigeon flight is less swift than teal but faster than mallard and, as the wings beat, the tips show below the outline of the body. Like mallard and teal, the wigeon is a surface feeder, so the ideal flight pond should have sloping sides and shallow feeding areas that are not more than 9in (22cm) deep.

You may occasionally see an American wigeon, which is similar in appearance to the English variety. The American wigeon would normally never be seen in this country were it not for the fact that the bird sometimes escapes from a domestic waterfowl collection.

GADWALL

The gadwall is another surface feeder, similar in movement to the mallard. The female has a more 'peaked' forehead and more pointed wings than the mallard. Apart from in Cumbria, Gloucestershire, Surrey, East Anglia and the Essex coast, the gadwall is a rather scarce and local winter visitor.

SHOVELLER

The rather large bill of the shoveller gives it an ungainly appearance while in flight. When it feeds the drake's unique yellow eye can often be seen from a considerable distance. When it swims, it is most often seen with its head well forward and the spoon-shaped bill touching the surface.

Together with most other waterfowl species, especially

those which feed on the surface, the shoveller is gregarious and mixes well with mallard, teal and wigeon.

TUFTED DUCK

In common with most diving ducks, the tufted duck has a more rapid and 'whirring' flight than any of the surface feeders. When it attempts to take off from water, it gives the appearance of paddling out of the water like a moorhen instead of jumping up and taking immediate flight in the manner of a mallard.

From a distance, the drake can be identified by its strongly contrasting black upper parts and white flanks. In some parts of the country, wildfowlers tend to know the tufted duck by the name of 'golden-eye'.

GOLDEN-EYE DUCK

The true golden-eye duck is larger than the tufted duck and the drake has a noticeable white spot on its face. Normally only seen on coastal and estuarine waters, this diving sea duck is sometimes found on large inland lakes, reservoirs and rivers.

Unlike the tufted duck, the golden-eye rises more directly from the water when it is disturbed and its wings make a loud singing or whistling note. Vocally, it is normally silent; only the duck gives a 'guttural grunt'.

POCHARD

The pochard is often found feeding and associating with tufted duck and hybrids between the two species are not uncommon. Unlike the golden-eye, pochard are rarely seen in or around areas of sea water and are generally more dumpy in appearance than either the tufted duck or the golden-eye. Shape is often the only way of identifying the bird in flight as it does not appear to possess any other distinguishing characteristics.

PINTAIL DUCK

This surface feeder needs no description when it is swimming as its name admirably describes its pointed and elongated tail, which is noticeable to even the most amateur of naturalists. The pintail can also be picked out from among other ducks by its white breast, although it should be noted that the drake shoveller has the same characteristic.

In flight, the pintail resembles the wigeon, but it is normally a little faster and, although the drake is normally silent, it occasionally emits a noise similar to a moorhen. The pintail's habitat and its flocking tendencies are also similar to those of the wigeon and at first glance the females of the two species are identical. On closer inspection, however, the pintail can be distinguished by its narrower wings and brown belly.

CANADA GOOSE

The Canada goose is probably the most common of the four species of goose at which one is allowed to shoot and it can be seen on waters throughout almost the whole of the United Kingdom. Surprisingly, most of today's resident population of Canada geese are a result of escapees from private collections over the last two hundred years, although occasionally genuine transatlantic migrants are shot.

Similar to the barnacle goose (which is fully protected), the Canada goose can be distinguished by its larger size, longer neck and smaller white face patch – information which can only prove useful when the two are seen side by side. A more positive indicator is that the barnacle goose hardly ever ventures inland.

In flight, the Canada goose is very noisy, giving out a loud honking described in the *Collins Guide to British Birds* as 'ker-honk'.

GREYLAG GOOSE

The main distinguishing features of the greylag are its relatively heavy, farmyard goose-like build, mannerisms and flight. Its orange beak and pink legs are unique among types of grey goose.

Its identification will probably cause problems only to the most ardent of wildfowlers who travel to Scotland, the Solway Firth and the Washes in search of their sport, because in other parts of the country it is only a sporadic winter visitor which is most likely to be seen during or immediately after a prolonged period of hard weather.

PINK-FOOTED AND WHITE-FRONTED GEESE

The greylag, pink-footed and white-fronted goose are all grey birds; all have a white tail with a dark centre and both the pink-footed and the white-fronted have white foreheads. It is not surprising therefore that the *Collins Guide to British Birds* sees the grey geese as presenting 'one of the hardest problems of field identification for beginners' and suggests a visit to the Wildfowl Trust at Slimbridge.

One basic point to remember (always supposing that you are close enough to see) is to look at the colour of the beak and feet: an orange beak and pink feet identify a greylag, whereas a pink beak and pink feet indicate a pink-foot. A pink bill and orange legs, or orange bill and orange legs, generally indicate that the bird is a white-front, which is also the only species to have no grey forewing, this being uniform with the rest of the upper parts.

Both the pink-footed and the white-fronted species have a more high-pitched cry than the greylag and both have a habit of flocking with each other rather than mixing with any of the other grey geese.

Bearing in mind the various problems of identification, I think that wildfowlers who are prepared to take the trouble to learn all they can before venturing out on the marshes and are then content to enjoy the sight of a dramatic sunrise or sunset and shoot a couple of ducks or a single goose, are very specialised and dedicated, especially if you take into account the cost of the camouflage, clothing and the correct background necessary for a successful outing.

Everyone – whether they intend to shoot wildfowl, pigeons, rabbits or game birds – should consider the fact that it is in their own interest to be able to name an individual species by its most obvious characteristics of colour, size, shape, flight and habit and, in the interests of the future well-being of the sport, to abide by their own voluntary laws and those which are decided by parliamentary decree.

8
Game Pie

Although not perhaps the most original of chapter titles, the above heading nevertheless aptly describes the many and varied contents, some of which, as in the making of a true game pie, should perhaps be taken with a pinch of salt.

The shooting world is full of characters and friendly faces. Even when the individual Gun has gone alone as a guest of an acquaintance, or has bought a day with a friend from an agency, it is very unlikely that he will return home or to his hotel without having spent a good part of the day talking and laughing with like-minded sportsmen.

Shooting is not just a matter of standing forward and shattering driven birds into oblivion. Without a full and interesting social side, it is doubtful whether many shooters would be tempted into the circle, and if they were, once they became competent killers, they would soon become bored.

I have seen some excellent Guns, known nationally for their prowess with a gun, sit for the best part of a drive without firing a shot because there had not been a sufficiently testing bird over them and yet they have enjoyed their day immensely because it took them away from the pressures of business and put them among like-minded people.

It must be said, however, that much of the fun comes from the keepers and beaters and it can be an education to be present in an old barn while they sit and talk over a packet of sandwiches and a can of beer, when the restraints of dining-room etiquette are absent. One thing is absolutely certain: there will be no shortage of amusing anecdotes and one man who has more than his fair share is Mr Henry Grass who, for many years, was head-keeper to the Earl Mountbatten of Burma. His Northumbrian accent adds to any tale, but his best story, in my opinion, was how he kept poachers at bay with his ferocious dog.

The first sign that all was not well for the local poachers came when a couple of workmen informed the pub's inhabitants of the arrival of Henry's new dog. They had been working at the head-keeper's house and asked for a shed in which they could eat their lunch. 'Certainly,' said Mr Grass, 'eat in there but, whatever you do, don't go near the door of *that* shed. I've just bought a new guard dog and he's too dangerous to be kennelled next to my others.'

Two or three days later, Henry happened to damage his forearm while working with a chainsaw. The bandaged arm caused much comment among the local inhabitants and, upon enquiry, they were told that the wounds had been caused by the 'new dog'. Local children were told not to reach into the back of the Land-Rover and attempt to stroke the muzzled dog which accompanied its owner on his trips into Romsey.

It was at least two seasons before the local poaching fraternity began to realise that no one had seen any dog other than the one in the vehicle and, had anyone investigated further, they would have noticed that this was only the same gentle old labrador that accompanied Henry on shooting days. The whole story was, in fact, an elaborate hoax which had developed from a series of incidents.

While it is obvious that there were always plenty of pheasants on the ground during his time as head-keeper, it is difficult to believe one of Mr Grass's other tales about when he was keepering in the North. According to him, so many birds were released that, in order to provide enogh roosting, it was necessary for the keepering staff to take out long poles each evening and push roosting pheasants closer together in an effort to make room for others still on the ground. Rabbits were also rather numerous; indeed, there were apparently so many that it was necessary to remove one or two rabbits from the hole before entering a ferret.

There is no doubt that Mr Grass met many famous people during the time he was head-keeper at Broadlands, but there are many others, notably in the Edwardian era, who became famous within the shooting world either because of their eccentricities or unbelievable skill with a 12 bore.

Shooting personalities of yesteryear

The person who is new to the shooting scene may hear some names mentioned during lunchtime conversations and be expected to know all about them, and it is in an effort to help with their education that I include the following.

Sir Ralph Payne Gallwey was, next to the king himself and his son the Prince of Wales, probably the most famous and accomplished figure to grace the large Edwardian shoots. Although he was an excellent pheasant shot, he is perhaps best remembered today for his love of wildfowling. As well as writing books on related subjects, he was also a compulsive inventor and he designed objects as diverse as gun-cleaning kits and cross-bows. For the last twenty years of his life, he lived at Thirkleby Hall in North Yorkshire, a place of particular interest to me as it was very close to where I began my keepering career and a game card designed by Payne Gallwey himself was a memento kept in the head-keeper's sideboard – a legacy from his father.

Not quite so well known, but none the less an interesting character, was the Marquess of Hartington, a predecessor of the present Duke of Devonshire (Chatsworth House). His nickname has become almost a household word and I well remember my mother describing other people's appalling taste in home furnishings or my own attempts to look suave and sophisticated for a night out as being 'arty-tarty'. It was not until reading *The Big Shots* by Jonathan Ruffer (an excellent book and one well worth adding to the Christmas list) that I realised that it was the name 'Harty Tarty' given to Lord Hartington by his fellow socialites, which had probably led to this saying. It resulted from his reputation of always being appallingly dressed: apparently, even when wearing the orders and decorations so necessary in entertaining foreign dignitaries of the day, he could not be relied upon to wear them the right way up.

Well before the Edwardian 'big shots', but still tenuously connected because Ralph Payne Gallwey edited a shortened edition of his *Instructions to Young Sportsmen*, came Colonel Peter Hawker. Hawker showed great tact in writing his celebrated book and, although it was addressed to youth, in reality his aims were to educate the whole of the shooting world. By treating the young and ignorant alike, he achieved the happy balance of instructing those who felt that they were beyond the learning stage as he would someone who had picked up a gun for the first time. The reader felt that he was being treated as an equal, no matter what status he had previously acquired.

Because the last two editions of his book were revised and published by his son, *Instructions to Young Sportsmen* proved to be the bible to any aspiring shooter for well over half a century and covered the dramatic change from flint-locks to the style of gun still in use today.

When perfected, these new guns brought about some major developments in the sport of shooting. They were quicker to reload, which meant a tremendous increase in the numbers of pheasants and partridges required and it was no longer possible to walk up game with the aid of dogs. More keepers were employed and their job was to fill their employer's estates to saturation point with artificially reared game until, in the heyday of Edwardian shooting, it was not uncommon for daily bags of three thousand pheasants.

There is often some confusion between Lord Walsingham and another excellent shot of the time, the Marquess of Ripon, both of whom were known by the surname 'de Grey'.

The Marquess of Ripon appeared to have had very little interest in anything other than shooting and was invited to all the great shoots because of his ability with a gun. I read in a magazine article that once, when shooting with the king at Sandringham, Lord Ripon killed twenty-eight pheasants in a minute and on another occasion had seven birds dead in the air at once. Obviously, loaders would have been necessary but, nevertheless, the speed at which he could shoot must have been incredible. In some fifty years of shooting, his game records show that he killed an astonishing 556,813 head of game, including (in 1882) two rhinoceros!

Record bags

On the Elveden shoot in Suffolk, the Maharajah Duleep Singh accounted for 780 partridge to his own gun in a single day. The record for the number of grouse shot in a single day by one person is 1,070 and it was achieved by Lord Walsingham at Blubberhouse Moor in Yorkshire when he made detailed plans which allowed almost every grouse on the moor to be driven over him by numerous teams of beaters. The whole operation was said to have taken fourteen hours and eighteen minutes.

A more modest game book appears in *The Wild Sports and Natural History of the Highlands*, written by Charles St John in 1863. A total of forty-three head was killed by St John on 21 October and the contents ranged from grouse to plover.

Although a keen sportsman, St John was also an observer and therefore an excellent naturalist and it is through his interest in the latter subject that his name is still well known today. Most of his days were spent on the moorlands of Scotland or by the river, although he was born in Sussex and educated at Midhurst.

Distance appeared to be no object when a shoot was in the offing and St John would think nothing of riding out of London on a round trip of 80 miles (128km) to shoot black-cock. (Where are black-cock to be found 40 miles (64km) from London today?)

A contemporary wrote of Charles St John:

> As a sportsman, his fire and eagerness were extreme; and he was especially fond of seeing his dogs work as he shot, never taking life merely for the wantonness of killing. But fishing and shooting were always subordinate to his ardour for observing the habits of the wild creatures which he possessed so many opportunities of noting. He insisted on seeing with his own eyes, and never cared to take facts on hearsay.

This ability to observe will help the modern Gun to compile his game book at the end of the day.

Keeping a game book

A game book or register should not merely contain a list of figures. It should be everyone's intention to emulate Charles St John's qualities of observation and spend some time after each outing in filling in the 'Remarks' column as fully as possible. Any appropriate photographs and drawings could be included and it may pay to pencil in some rough sketches of the way some drives were carried out.

There are several reasons for doing this. The first is the creation of a personal record of your sporting activities which can be dipped into in future years so that enjoyable experiences can be relived. Secondly, the keeper will find it useful to refer to his game records on the odd occasion when his employer has asked for a good day when a specific amount of birds could be expected in the bag. (Although bag numbers should be immaterial, there are times when a good day is essential – for instance, when an important business client is being entertained.) By looking back over previous years, certain drives which are known to produce good numbers of birds can be included. It would be a poor keeper who could not tell his employer which woods to drive without having to refer to his notes first, but the fact that one drive, pushed in the right direction, could help in filing pheasants towards a drive to follow lunch may be forgotten without the previously (possibly accidental) successful sequence being documented.

Thirdly, such records could prove to be of great interest to bodies committed to the future well-being of this country's wildlife. The Game Conservancy for example, have for many years carried out a National Game Census and they need untold sets of records gathered from estates throughout the country so that they can build up a general picture, the results of which are published in their annual members' review.

In the period 1986–7, the Game Conservancy's research was able to prove that there was a noticeable upward trend in the number of returns from pheasants released in southern England, which were almost on a level with those noted in 1984 – the highest yet recorded. In the same season, more red-legged partridges were reared and shot than in any previously recorded year and it was possible for the Conservancy to establish that the hand-rearing of partridges (red-legs) had increased almost thirtyfold in the south, but in East Anglia the rates were 'sixty times as high as they were in the early seventies'.

Finally, a detailed game book could be of benefit to future generations and, should the shooting of game birds ever be banned by a non-sporting government, it will be a historical document about some of today's leisure activities.

Game books

A good quality bound and printed game book will cost upwards of £35 but, in my opinion, it is money well spent and the book will last the average sportsman at least ten years.

The Game Conservancy offers for sale *The Personal Sporting Almanac* in which there are well designed pages on fine quality paper to cater for the shooter, fisherman, deer stalker, hunting enthusiast or equestrian eventer, and special pages for photos, notes and a year planner. It all binds up into a fine morocco leather or buckram bound volume – a permanent record of your sport. The price at the end of the 1987–8 season was £29.95 plus postage and packing.

David & Charles offer *The Country Sportsman's Record Book and Journal*, current price £20. It contains beautiful colour illustrations and quotes from many famous fieldsports personalities and is ideal for personal records and reminiscences of sporting days.

Poachers

One topic which always seems to interest visitors on a shooting day is the subject of poachers. What every Gun should realise is that poachers are no longer (if they ever were) cringing farm labourers with six children to support, looking for a single pheasant or a rabbit in order to give the family meat on a Sunday. Poaching today is big business and, for some, it is a profession.

The following may seem too much of a coincidence to be true but, halfway through writing the last sentence, I broke off to answer a telephone call from a keepering colleague who rang to tell me that he had once again had trouble with poachers. It was mid-September so they were obviously after deer as the newly released pheasants could only be passed off (plucked and dressed) as partridge.

In this instance, the poachers' vehicle was an ex-Electricity Board van, bought cheaply at a car auction. A service van offers poachers the opportunity to cruise around the countryside without rousing suspicion. In this way, the poachers had every opportunity to assess the haunts of the deer stocks and, if it was not practicable to take an animal immediately, the time was not wasted as it made their return with lurchers and lamps that much more likely to be successful.

The old adage of pheasant shooters still applies: 'Up goes a guinea, bang goes a shilling and down comes half a crown.' Taking inflation and decimalisation into account, it might today read 'Up goes £15, bang goes 10p and down comes £1.50'. That brief sentence highlights the huge cost of rearing and releasing a bird, the minor expense of a cartridge and the price you can expect as a return on dead game. Therefore, for a poacher to make a living from his nefarious exploits, if he only concentrated on pheasants he would need to take so many birds that he would not be able to carry them.

For this reason, deer of one type of another seem to be favoured quarry and even a small roe is worth perhaps £30 to a butcher or irresponsible game dealer.

In an effort to tighten up on deer poaching, new laws were invoked a few years ago which should have ensured that only legitimately killed animals were offered for sale. The dealer to whom they are sold is supposed to make sure that he knows exactly from which estate they originate and, if they are intended for export, each carcase should be tagged, marked and logged. Unfortunately, it is all too easy to sell any type of game to unscrupulous dealers or to butchers and hoteliers who are prepared not to ask too many questions provided that the price is right.

Hares are another species which attract the attention of poachers but, in the majority of cases, it is not for the price which can be had for the dead animal but as a means of testing the individual's lurcher against another with vast sums of money being betted on the most likely winner of the course.

Although the price given for pheasants makes their poaching less attractive, nevertheless some estates suffer extensively from visits by poachers who feel that the birds are still worth the effort. It is not just that birds which have been carried away by poachers obviously cannot be driven over the Guns which worries the keeper but also, when pheasants are roosting in and around the release pens at the beginning of the season, there is a good chance that many others will be disturbed during the raid and will fly off into the darkness. It is unlikely that they will land in neighbouring trees and instead will merely 'jug' on the ground, giving the resident foxes an easy meal. When morning comes, those which have survived the night will probably be somewhat disorientated and are just as likely to wander off over the boundary as they are to return home.

An efficient gang can clear a wood, shooting roosting birds with torch and gun. One shoots while the others gather and carry away the birds. As I mentioned earlier, many pheasants are required to make a night's work worthwhile but, with careful planning, it can be done.

Some keepers take the law into their own hands and, in recent years, there has been a disturbing increase in the number of horrific injuries and serious assaults on keepers. No matter how good an employer you might have, loyalty should stop short of confronting a gang of poachers on your own. Discretion is definitely the better part of valour and it is a sensible keeper who merely pinpoints the intruders' location, the whereabouts of their vehicle and its make, registration number and colour before contacting the police.

Technology has come to the keeper's aid and he can be warned of the presence of poachers by means of radio transmitters and receivers. The beams of electronic sensors can usually be made to cross a ride, narrowly and flat edged so that on level ground they can be set up to detect a man passing through without giving false alarms when deer or other forms of wildlife pass underneath.

Some water authorities have purchased image intensifiers similar to those used by the armed services and, as a result, their bailiffs have brought about several successful prosecutions.

The average shoot will not be able to do much more than equip his keeper with a CB radio fitted to his vehicle.

When setting up any form of poacher detector device, it is essential to ensure that beams, pressure pads or any other activating system are situated well above the height at which deer or other wildlife will accidentally alarm the keeper

This can be a very effective means of allowing the keeper to contact home so that a telephone call can be made to the local police while the keeper remains at a crucial observation point. However, CBs are readily available and cheap so that poachers, too, may be similarly equipped and can listen to what the keeper has to say.

The poaching fraternity definitely does not include the worldy-wise cottager, wearing old tweeds, ferrets in the pocket, travelling the fields and woodlands in an effort to feed his wife and uncountable brood of children, robbing from the rich to give to the poor. Instead, poachers are more likely to be city raised, unscrupulous and violent, deserving no sympathy but the harshest of prison sentences.

The effects of wet weather on the shooting day

A visit from poachers the previous night could provide the keeper with an excellent excuse when there is a shortage of birds to put over the Guns, but a better one, to my mind, is to blame adverse weather conditions.

Rain and snow can literally dampen the spirits of even the most enthusiastic of Guns and I have heard beaters on wet and windy days say to each other, 'I'm glad I'm beating and keeping warm – wouldn't like to be a Gun standing out there in all this.'

Unpleasant though shooting in such conditions is for the Gun, it can spell absolute disaster to the keeper. If he is in charge of game on a small family shoot where only eight or nine days are planned in a season, a wet or snowy day could completely spoil certain drives and lower the season's returns.

After a wet and windy night, the shooting day can take one of two courses. If the early morning is bright and sunny, the pheasants will rapidly leave the cold, wet woodland in favour of a sunny hedgerow where they will be lost, unless a couple of beaters are delegated to bring in that hedgerow towards the main drive. Several drives like this will obviously reduce the number of birds one would otherwise normally expect to see. On such a morning, it is not safe even to assume that any cover crops will produce a good showing of game, because if the crop is mainly kale or another broad-leaved variety, the cover could prove to be wetter than the woods in which the birds roost.

On the other hand, a damp morning, full of drizzle rather than heavy rain, can pay handsome dividends. The first drive in these circumstances will almost undoubtedly be successful because the pheasants have not yet left home, but the rest of the day will depend upon the keeper's astuteness and the correct positioning of 'stops' to prevent escapees from other drives joining in. The keeper or person in charge of the line should also remember not to run birds too far through wet undergrowth or cover crops as this will lessen the chances of producing a high-flying, sporting bird. A pheasant with wet feathers cannot fly as well as it would normally.

After a fall of snow, there is a tendency among keepers to rush out eagerly to their feed rides expecting the hard weather to have driven birds back into the woods. Instead, the rides are often bare with very little in the way of pheasant footprints. It seems that, until they become used to it, the birds are unsure of their new environment and remain under cover. Anyone with a few free-range chickens will no doubt have noticed their reluctance to put a foot out of the hen-house for some time in snow and the same is no doubt true with pheasants.

Expecting a successful shooting day immediately after a heavy fall of snow will result in some very frustrated and disappointed Guns. Because of the birds' reluctance to travel, it is impossible to whistle them from the roosting woods to the areas from which they are to be driven. Even in places where pheasants are known to be contained in great numbers, it will be a difficult job to get them out and over the Guns because they sit so tightly and are either walked over by the beaters or 'pegged' by their dogs. If you are successful in getting the odd bird to fly, it will probably not fly all that well because it will be disorientated by the vast white expanse.

Negative and positive ions can have an effect on the performance of pheasants and their normal behaviour can sometimes be disrupted by low-frequency electromagnetic wave fronts which precede stormy weather. These atmospheric disturbances disrupt the inbuilt electromagnetic compass which all birds contain in their heads, and cause disorientation and confused behaviour.

In other situations, a disappointing day may have nothing to do with weather conditions but will be due entirely to the fact that wind direction, noise from Guns and beaters and the importance of stops have not been taken into consideration.

Justifying the sport of shooting

It would be presumptuous to attempt to put forward an argument which the reader can then use as a retort to those who disagree with the morals of shooting animals and birds for sport. We all have our reasons and those should be enough to justify our indulgence.

In my book *Beagling* (David & Charles, 1987), I said:

> 'For someone to actually enjoy killing for the sake of it seems to them [the 'antis'] to be totally unacceptable. If beaglers ventured into the field merely to see a hare caught and killed, then their morals and mentality must indeed be in question.

The same applies to shooting or, indeed, fishing and I hope that in the preceding chapters I have shown that there is more to field sports than killing. The reader who has participated in any form of shooting already knows this and will probably cite the fact that his sport allows him to escape from business pressures and provides fresh air and companionship. If his interest extends as far as training a gun-dog, that is a hobby in itself and although after a particularly bad session the trainer may go to bed worried and despondent at his pupil's lack of progress, in the morning he will awake with a new way of overcoming the obstacle and his summer evenings will be spent ironing out faults in readiness for the coming season.

Perhaps the greatest argument in favour of the continuation of shooting is that it effectively aids conservation. Without the need to manage habitat in order to ensure that game has a fair chance of survival and that pheasants will be where required on a shooting day, it would not be long before hedgerows had grown tall and contained no bottom. Woodland canopies would soon prevent sunlight from reaching the forest floor, causing the death of undergrowth, and the only form of wildlife would be predator species, notably magpies.

If shooting was ever banned, there would be no incentive for anyone to manage the countryside, unless countryside wardens were employed as civil servants. Admittedly, 'conservation' groups have never been stronger, but the average member seems to live with a sadly mis-conceived idea of Utopia, thinking that nature left alone, will somehow muddle through.

Nature needs a helping hand: effective conservation rarely comes from a meeting in the village hall. In controlling predators such as crows, magpies, rats and weasels, a wide range of songbirds will benefit as well as game. Winter feeding will save many a small bird from starvation and I have seen them answer to my feed whistle quicker than the pheasants.

Helping wildlife

Cutting a large wood in two immediately provides eight sides rather than four and, as most forms of wildlife favour woodland edges, rather than its centre, such action can only be beneficial.

The grouse shooter, by means of his willingness to pay vast sums for his sport, has already aided the survival of moorland and its place as an upland reserve for many birds of prey and plants. There is much publicity in the media decrying the increasing use of moorland for softwood timber plantations and it is only the united front shown by grouse shooters which has prevented the encroachment of coniferous afforestation.

The future of shooting

There is increasing pressure on the countryside now that EEC directives are forcing the majority of farmers to change their attitudes and look for alternative means of income.

Fieldsports of any type must never be considered in isolation but the fact that the government is actively encouraging tree planting by offering grants to those who wish to plant broad-leaved species must mean more habitat is available in which to release pheasants. By charging those who wish to shoot, the landowner increases his annual income – an important fact when you realise that areas planted up for forestry immediately lose their value with regard to land prices. Fields of grass or arable land are more attractive to a potential buyer than are acres of woodland.

With the increasing awareness of the importance of personal bodily health coupled with more leisure time, there is bound to be an upsurge in the need for long-distance footpaths, and links are already being planned for footpaths and bridleways. This is not necessarily good news for the shooter who may find that, as a result, the release pen situated near a well-used track is continually disturbed by those of an inquisitive nature who are accompanied by free-ranging dogs.

Building of any form is likely to meet with a great deal of opposition among country dwellers. Parliament has already admitted that there is likely to be less money available to be spent in rural communities. Country dwellers need to find alternatives, but there is bound to be a limit to demand, whatever use is found. Organic farming could be on the increase but eventually it will require just as much funding as do the artificial methods in use today. An imposed 'fallow' system will restrict the growth of corn but the farmer will need, and indeed expect, some form of compensation.

The only plus factor to come from this change of land use whereby the public can come into closer contact with landowners and farmers, is the greater emphasis on the need for co-operation between landowners and casual countryside users. If, during the course of conversation, points can be put forward which explain and justify the future of field sports in general and game shooting in particular, so much the better.

The importance of field sports in connection with the national economy was brought to the fore in 1983, following certain vote-catching political attacks on our traditional recreation, by the report of the Standing Conference on Countryside Sports. However, Guns can no longer expect the countryside to provide them with exclusive facilities for hunting, shooting and fishing.

If this book helps Guns to rub along with other users, to enable them to find pleasure from their own particular sport, or explains the many problems which have to be overcome before shooting becomes a justifiable sporting activity, or nudges the more experienced person to remember etiquette and safety learnt earlier in life, then my efforts will not have been wasted and I am certain that shooting will continue to provide excellent relaxation without adding fuel to the fire of those who wish to see it terminated.

Useful Addresses

Sporting Hotels
The Lake Vyrnwy Hotel, via Oswestry, Shropshire SY10 0LY
The Salston Hotel, Ottery St Mary, Exeter, Devon EX11 1RQ
The Arundell Arms, Lifton, Devon PL16 0AA

For Ireland contact:
Irish Tourist Board, Baggot Street Bridge, Dublin 2 (Tel: 0001-765871)

NB The *Shooting Times* magazine offers occasional comprehensive guides to British sporting holidays.

Sporting Agencies
Cowley Shooting Associates Ltd, Woodland Head, Yeoford, Crediton, Devon
Hawkeye Sporting Agency, (Mike Manley), Keeper's Cottage, Bighton, Arlesford, Hampshire

Sporting Properties For Sale (**in Scotland**)
A.W.M. Fletcher, Mains of Balavil, Kingussie, Inverness-shire PH21 1LU

Time-share Shooting
Savills, 46 Charlotte Square, Edinburgh EH2 4HQ

Gun Distributors
ASI, Alliance House, Snape, Saxmundham, Suffolk IP17 1SW
Browning Sports Ltd, 37d Milton Trading Estate, Milton, Abingdon, Oxfordshire OX14 4RT
Leslie Hewett Ltd, Upton Cross, Liskeard, Cornwall PL14 5BQ

The Gun Trade Association Ltd will also be able to assist in acquiring further addresses. The association is based at: Fairbourne Cottage, Bunny Lane, Timsbury, Romsey, Hampshire SO51 0PG

Rifles (**and shotgun repairs**)
G.E. Fulton & Son, Bisley Ranges, Brookwood, Woking, Surrey

Clothing Manufacturers
Cambrian Flyfishers, The Old Vicarage, Trevor, Llangollen, North Wales LL20 7YR
John Maile Ltd, Church Norton, Selsey, Chichester, West Sussex
John Norris (specialists in Barbour clothing) 21 Victoria Road, Penrith, Cumbria CA11 8HP

Gun-dogs
Any sporting magazine (especially *Shooting Times*) contains the addresses of some of the more established kennels which specialise in the training of gun-dogs; therefore, it is only necessary to include the address of the country's leading manufacturer of gun-dog training equipment:
Turner-Richards, Cardigan Street, Birmingham B4 7SA

General Keepering Requisites

Youngs, Enterprise Works, Crewkerne, Missterton, Somerset

Gilbertson & Page, Corrys, Roestock Lane, Colney Heath, Herts AL4 0QH

Farming and Wildlife Advisory Group, The Lodge, Sandy, Bedfordshire SG19 2DL

Forestry Commission, Sherwood Forest District Office, Edwinstowe, Mansfield, Nottinghamshire

Game Conservancy, Burgate Manor, Fordingbridge, Hampshire SP6 1EF

Nature Conservancy Council, North Minster House, Peterborough PE1 1UA

St Hubert Club, The Apes Hall, Littleport, Ely, Cambridgeshire

Scottish Landowners' Federation, 18 Abercromby Place, Edinburgh EH3 6TY

William Evans, 67a St James Street, London SW1A 1PH

James Purdey & Sons Ltd, Audley House, 57–8 South Audley Street, London W1Y 6ED

General Addresses

British Association for Shooting and Conservation, Marford Mill, Rossett, Clwyd LL12 0HL

British Deer Society, Church Farm, Lower Basildon, Reading, Berkshire RG8 9NH

British Field Sports Society, 59 Kennington Road, London SE1 7PZ

Clay Shooting Association, 107 Epping New Road, Buckhurst Hill, Essex IG9 5TQ (also supplies the addresses of various shooting schools)

Country Landowners Association, Icknield Way West, Letchworth, Hertfordshire SG6 4AP

Game-shooting Videos

Holland & Holland *Shooting Times, The Definitive Instruction Video,* Prospectus Game Shooting, Box 44, Leatherhead, Surrey KT22 7AE

James Douglas: *Koebuck Stalking, Training Spaniels, Red*

Deer Stalking, Training the Labrador Retriever, the Wild-fowler, The Sporting Shotgun – Wildtrack Video Ltd, Hunter Street, Auchterarder, Perthshire PH3 1PA

Game Shooting Abroad
Selous Hunters, Horsted Keynes, West Sussex RH17 7AJ

Best London Gunmakers
Holland & Holland, 33 Bruton Street, London W1X 8JS
James Purdey & Sons Ltd, Audley House, 57–8 South Audley Street, London W1Y 6ED

Sporting Press
Country Life, King's Reach Tower, Stamford Street, London SE1 9LS
Countrysport, Wharncliffe House, Church Street, Barnsley, South Yorkshire
The Field Carmelite House, Carmelite Street, London EC4
Shooting Times and Country Magazine, 10 Sheet Street, Windsor, Berkshire
Sporting Gun, Bretton Court, Bretton, Peterborough, Cambridgeshire

Bibliography

Beaumont, Richard, *Shotgun and Cartridges* (A. & C. Black, 4th ed, paperback, 1987)
Fitter, R.S.R., and Richardson, R.A., *Collins Pocket Guide to British Birds* (Collins, 1952)
Hastings, Macdonald, *Shotgun* (David & Charles, 1981)
Hawker, Lt Col P., *Instructions to Young Sportsmen* (republished by W.J. Ward, 1975)
Martin, Brian P., *Sporting Birds of the British Isles* (David & Charles, 1984, reprinted 1986)
The Great Shoots (David & Charles, 1987)
Moxon, P.R.A., *Gundogs* (Popular Dogs, 14th ed, 1986)
Parkes, Charles, and Thornley, John, *Fair Game* (Pelham, 1987)
Ruffer, J.E.M., *Good Shooting* (David & Charles, 1980)
Ruffer, J.G., *The Big Shots* (Debretts, 4th ed, 1979)
Thomas, Gough, *Shotgun and Cartridges* (A & C Black, 4th ed paperback, 1987)

Acknowledgements

The author would like to offer his grateful thanks to the following:

The estate of Brian Vesey-Fitzgerald and Laurence Pollinger Ltd for permission to quote from *British Game*. Anne Voss-Bark, The Arundell Arms. Niels and Sally Svendsen, The Salston Hotel. Nicola Bisiker and the proprietors of the Lake Vyrnwy Hotel. Terry Cowley of Cowley Shooting Associates. Mike Manley of Hawkeye Sporting Agency. Special thanks to Inspector Michael Bardwell and PC Hugh Hubbard for sorting out some of the relevant game laws included in Chapter 7. Richard Northcott for permission to photograph on his estates. Gina Arnold, 'Dick' Hedger, Graham Simpson and my father for their excellent photographs. Clare Pavey for once again agreeing to supply some superb line drawings, despite my bullying and criticism. Richard Clark-Hall for sharing knowledge gained from a lifetime of shooting. Dave O'Connell for always knowing the right addresses.

Index